VENEERING:
A FOUNDATION COURSE

MIKE BURTON

Sterling Publishing Co., Inc.

New York

Library of Congress Cataloging-in-Publication Data

Burton, Mike, 1944-
Veneering : a foundation course / Mike Burton.
p. cm.
Includes index.
ISBN 1-4027-2649-X
1. Veneers and veneering. I. Title.

TS870.B87 2006
674'.833—dc22
2005019151

Published by Sterling Publishing Co., Inc.
387 Park Avenue South, New York, NY 10016
© 2000, 2006 by Mike Burton
Based on a previously published edition
Distributed in Canada by Sterling Publishing
c/o Canadian Manda Group, 165 Dufferin Street
Toronto, Ontario, Canada M6K 3H6
Distributed in the United Kingdom by GMC Distribution Services
Castle Place, 166 High Street, Lewes, East Sussex, England BN71XU
Distributed in Australia by Capricorn Link (Australia) Pty. Ltd.
P.O. Box 704, Windsor, NSW 2756, Australia

Sterling ISBN 13: 978-1-4027-2649-1
ISBN 10: 1-4027-2649-X

For information about custom editions, special sales, premium and
corporate purchases, please contact Sterling Special Sales
Department at 800-805-5489 or specialsales@sterlingpub.com.

CONTENTS

 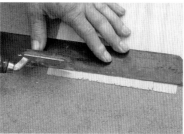 

Introduction 8
Safety Considerations 10

PART 1 ALL ABOUT VENEER 11

CHAPTER 1:

From Log to Workshop: Cutting
  Characteristics of Veneer 12
Reasons for Using Veneer 13
How Veneer is Cut 14
Care After Slicing 17
How Veneer is Supplied 17
Paper-Backed Veneer 17
Cross-Banded Veneer 17
Veneer Presentations 18
Species Characteristics 20
  Oils and Resins 20
  End Checks, Splits, and Tears 20
  Thin and Thick Areas and
    Grain Holes 21
  Mineral Deposits 22
  Color Retention 22
  Holes 22
  Wrinkles 23
  Surface Compression and Checking 23
  Characteristics of Paper-Backed
    and Cross-Banded Veneers 24

CHAPTER 2:

Tools and Equipment 25
Cutting Tools 25
  Straightedges 25
  Knives with Disposable Blades 27
  Linoleum Knives 28
  Veneer Saws 28
  Modifying a Veneer Saw 29
  Rotary Cutters 31
  Paper Cutters 32
  Scissors and Snips 32
Cutting Surface 32
Carving Tools 32
Power Tools 33
Punches 33
  Patching Technique 34
Household Iron 36
Glue Containers with Spreaders 37
Toothed Spreaders 37
Layout Tools 39
  Scribing Dividers 39
  Edge Scribes 40

Circle Devices	40	Man-Made Boards	62
Veneer Hammers	41	Veneer-Core Plywood	63
Abrasive Devices	42	Lumber-Core Plywood	63
Clamps and Other Equipment	42	Apple/Maple and Baltic Birch	63
		Bender Board	63
		Particleboard	64
CHAPTER 3:		MDF (Medium-Density Fiberboard)	64
Preparing and Cutting Veneer	**43**	Fasteners and Water	64
Preparation	43	Other Substrates	65
Flattening Techniques	44	Metal	65
Minor Flattening	45	Glass	65
Flattening Veneer with a		Drywall	65
Household Iron	45	Layout Technique	65
Flattening Veneer with a Hot Press	46	Circles	65
Flattening Veneer with Water,		Ovals	66
Glycerin, and Alcohol	46	Irregular Curves	66
Flattening Veneer with Steam	47	Edge Treatments	67
Drying Technique	48	Solid Wood	67
Commonly Asked Questions	50	Plywood and Composition Boards	67
Strengthening Veneer	50	Round, Oval, and Other	
Taping for Added Strength	51	Irregular Edges	70
Sizing	51	Facings Thicker Than the Substrate	70
Bonding Veneer to a Backing	51	Applying Facing After the Substrate	
Dyeing Veneers	52	Has Been Veneered	71
Pre-Forming Veneer	52	Hinges, Locks, and Other	
Cutting Veneer	53	Hardware	71
Shooting	54	Shaping Composites	71
Taping Veneer Pieces	55	Trimming and Repairing	
Types of Tape	55	Faced Substrates	71
Applying Paper Tape	57	Final Procedures	72
Tape Removal	58		
CHAPTER 4:		**CHAPTER 5:**	
Substrates	**59**	**Bonding Veneer to the Substrate**	**73**
Pull	59	Adhesive Properties	73
Dealing with Pull	60	Strength of Bond	73
Pre-Cupping	60	Penetration	74
Sizing	60	Shock Resistance	74
Veneering Both Sides of the Substrate	60	Hardness	74
Telegraphing	61	Glue-Line Thickness	74
Wood Substrates to Avoid	61	Clamping Pressure	74
Solid Wood	61	Gap-Filling Properties	74

Open Assembly Time 75
Initial Adhesion or "Tack" 75
Setting Time/Drying Time 75
Susceptibility to Heat 76
Creep 76
Reversibility 76
Susceptibility to Solvents 76
(Including Water) 76
Types of Adhesive 76
Hot Hide Glue 76
Preparing Hot Hide Glue 78
Cleanup 79
An Experiment with Hot
Hide Glue 79
Liquid Hide Glue 80
PVA Glues 80
White Glue 80
Yellow Glue 81
Water-Resistant Yellow Glue 81
Urea-Formaldehyde 81
Mixing Technique 82
Cleanup 82
Contact Cement 82
Cleanup 84
Other Adhesive Possibilities 84
Bonding Techniques 84
Using a Hammer and Hide Glue 84
A Practice Session 85
Hammering with Other Adhesives 90
Hammering Irregular Shapes 91
Dry-Glue Bonding 91
Preparation 92
Bonding Techniques 93
Joints 94
Compressed Joints 94
Contact Cement 94
Bonding Using Mechanical Presses 96
Press Criteria 96
Things to Be Aware of When
Using the Press 96
The Effects of Heat 97

Cauling 98
Cauls Made From Waste 98
Molded Cauls 99
Bonding Using a Vacuum Press 99
Bonding Challenges 101
Detecting Loose Spots 102
Fixing Loose Spots 102
Dealing with Bubbles 103
Open Joints 103

CHAPTER 6:
Shop-Made Veneering Equipment and
Miscellaneous Techniques 104
Mechanical Veneering Press 104
Dimensions 104
Top 104
Base 104
Stock Preparation 105
Base 105
Top 105
Spanner Sticks 105
Assembly 105
Base 106
Top 106
Finishing Up 107
Press Heater 107
Solar Heater 107
Steam-"Fired" Heater 108
Cutting the Groove for the
Copper Tubing 108
Placing the Copper Tubing 109
Finishing Up 110
Fastening the Aluminum Plate 110
Operation 111
Other Applications 112
Steam Generator 114
Construction Details and
Instructions 115
Operation and Safety Precautions 116
Miscellaneous Veneering Techniques 117
Veneering Moldings 117

Veneering Turnings 117
Spiral Veneering 119

CHAPTER 7:

Adding a Finish 120
Patching 120
Sanding 120
Power Sanding 122
Altering the Color of Veneer 122
Pigmented Stains 122
Dye Stains 122
Combination Stains 123
Glazing Stains 124
Bleach 124
Fillers 125
Oil Finishes 125
Topcoats 126
Lacquer 126
Shellac and Varnish 126

Water-Based Topcoats 126
Overall Considerations 126

CHAPTER 8:

Marquetry 127
Reinforcing the Pieces 127
Cutting Curves 128
Adjusting Cuts 131
Cutting Techniques 131
Pattern-Cutting 131
Window-Cutting 131
Multi-Cutting 132
Pad-Cutting 133
Special Inlay Techniques 135
Shading 136

PART 2   PROJECTS   137

CHAPTER 9:

Simple Projects 138
Simple Box 138
Coasters 140
Checkerboard 144

CHAPTER 10:

Veneered Lamp 150
Pattern 150
Substrate (Ground) Preparation 150
Cutting the Blank 151
Preparing the Veneer 153
Veneering the First Two Surfaces 153
Final Procedures 154
Base 156

CHAPTER 11:

Veneered Blanket Chest	**158**
Veneer Layout and Taping	159
Pressing the Veneer	163
Chest Assembly	167
Adding a Finish	173

CHAPTER 12:

Kidney-Shaped Desk	**174**
Preparing the Form for the	
Curved Case	176
Layout	176
Cutting the Form	176
Working with the Form	177
Assembly	177
Preparing the Bender Board	179
Bending the Moldings	181
Trimming the Case	181
Drawer Fronts	181
Cutting the Legs	181
Drawer Compartments	181
Working with the Top	191
Adding a Finish	199

CHAPTER 13:

Round Dining Table	**200**
Preparing the Pedestal and Base	201
Pedestal	203
Base	203

Veneering the Base	207
Veneering the Pedestal	209
Building the Rim	209
Laying Out the Top	211
Veneering the Pedestal's Bead	213
Veneering the Top	213
Assembling the Base	216
Adding a Finish	216

CHAPTER 14:

Bombé Chest	**217**
Drawings and Patterns	217
Preparing the Components	221
Side Pieces	221
Legs	222
Finalizing the Case Sides	222
Gluing Back the Waste	222
Cutting the Side Scallop	224
Preparing the Lower Scalloped Rail	224
Preparing the Upper Rails	225
Assembly	227
Drawers	227
Shaping the Drawer Fronts	227
Veneering the Drawer Fronts	229
Veneering the Top	233
Making the Backing and Dust	
Protector	237
Adding a Finish	237

Index   238
Metric Equivalents Chart   240

INTRODUCTION

Many times I have been asked, "Where did you learn about veneering?" I usually mention my local public library. That's where my knowledge of veneering began and continues to this day, but through the years as a woodworker I have also had the opportunity and honor to watch and to work alongside some excellent craftsmen. Professionals all, these people built the project they were assigned with calm, step-by-step determination, filled with the pragmatism of the day.

I am not a hobbyist, and far too little of my work has ever found its way into my own home. I am a professional craftsman in several woodworking fields—which means I get paid for providing services in these fields. I have worked professionally in several crafts, and in this book I'll try to show some of the interrelated techniques I've learned through the years.

I received my first paid woodworking commission in 1962, and hung a shingle over the door of a woodworking shop in 1972; that shingle remains to this day. Through the years, that shop has engaged in a wide variety of woodworking-related enterprises, from general millwork to the cutting of dimensioned lumber to the manufacture of airplane propellers and guitar bodies to the production of custom furniture. In the following pages, I describe and show how some of the techniques I've learned through the years in these crafts can be applied to veneering.

Though the production of custom furniture has always been my goal, restoration and refinishing work have taken a great deal of my time. I'm thankful for that work, as it has given me the opportunity to study many pieces from different periods, evaluating what ensures a piece's longevity and what contributes to its demise. I have always been a tinker and experimenter—often to the dismay of my sons, who have worked with me. But my tinkering and experimenting have proven to be a great way to obtain an education in veneering.

If you are a student of general woodworking, some of the tools and techniques that are presented here may seem unconventional. Try them; they may work well for you. You don't have to tell your purest woodworking acquaintances about these unorthodox methods; I certainly won't.

One thing I've discovered is that there's no "right" way to do anything; nor is the "wrong" way always wrong. If the same project were assigned to five competent, professional woodworkers, they would probably take five different approaches to the task, but each finished product would be totally acceptable.

In the following pages, I take the reader step-by-step through the veneering process and describe and show how to build a variety of projects. I incorporate the veneering of flat surfaces along with curved surfaces in some rather unique pieces to present ideas on how to veneer even the simplest of projects. I've also used a number of different types of veneer for these projects that exhibit different properties.

I have dealt heavily with the veneering of curved surfaces, because many woodworkers think that these surfaces are the most difficult. It goes without saying that if you can veneer a curved surface, you can veneer a flat one.

Another reason for working with curved surfaces is that they lend themselves to veneer in a very special way. Economy is one reason, to be sure, but there are effects that can be arrived at on a curved veneered surface that could never be created with solid wood. A bombé chest—one with outward curving lines—or a curved desk always draws more

Author Mike Burton working on the blanket chest described in Chapter 11.

compliments than its counterparts with square components. (Both types of furniture are covered in Chapters 12 and 14.) And, as I work for profit rather than fun, I've found the financial rewards are also far greater, while the effort is about the same—honest.

When reading the project section, don't look at the finished product photo and say, "I could never do that." Look carefully at the in-progress shots and read the accompanying text. Think about the tools and materials you have at hand. Adapt my ideas to that special project that you've always wanted to try. Then roll up your sleeves and get to work.

Read on. Try some different techniques—even those that may be considered unusual. Don't practice these techniques on your project, but rather on scrap wood. Most of all, enjoy the experience.

MIKE BURTON

SAFETY CONSIDERATIONS

As you browse through the book and look at the photos, you'll see me working without eye protection or a dust mask while using a tool that generates a great deal of dust. With regard to dust, there are two large squirrel-cage fans in my workshop that circulate filtered air gently throughout it. The airflow clears fine dust in a matter of seconds. That said, keep in mind that although it is wonderful to work with many exotic species of woods, there are health risks. It is said that East Indian Rosewood is carcinogenic. It is possible to have severe allergic reactions to the dust of others. Use particle masks and a dust collection system.

And as for eye protection, although I often feel that it's as important to clearly see what I'm doing as it is to protect my eyes, you would be well advised to use goggles.

In the following pages, you'll see woodworking tools being used without safety gadgets and guards. This decision not to use the safety equipment is one I've made as a professional woodworker with years of experience, and the reader is advised to make his own decision based on his level of expertise and comfort level.

Finally, heed my specific safety precautions in the following pages.

PART **1** ALL ABOUT VENEER

CHAPTER 1

FROM LOG TO WORKSHOP: CUTTING CHARACTERISTICS OF VENEER

Veneering—the technique of overlaying material over wood for protective or decorative purposes—is not a new craft. Artifacts covered with veneer have been found in the tombs of the pharaohs. The term "veneer" does not solely refer to wood—although wood is the focus of this book. Stone, shells, and metals can also be used as veneers.

Until modern times—say, from 1900 on—veneered objects could be found only in the possession of the wealthy. The materials and talent to produce veneered pieces were beyond the means of the common man. Usually of exotic wood, often of unique design, and always elegant, veneered pieces were more appreciated by the well-to-do, for the common man was far more taken up with the practicalities of daily life.

In the area of furniture-making, veneer has been used a little differently during various time periods. During the Second World War there was a scarcity of good hardwood timber, glue—and craftsmen. But during that period, there was a fair amount of furniture produced. Not all, but a good deal of this furniture was built of vertical-grain fir and covered with veneer to disguise the not-so-appropriate lumber. Often the lumber was hastily cured and joints were poorly fit. As a result, far too many of these pieces fell apart of their own weight, finishes disintegrated, and veneers began to come loose. Consequently,

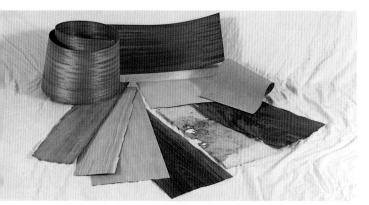

1-1. Different species of veneer.

Veneer Terminology

The following terms are used throughout this chapter. Familiarity with them will help you better understand the craft of veneering.

Book and Butt Match. The technique of flipping two slices of a stack of four burl slices and then turning the top ones end for end. This produces a pattern in which each slice touches in the center, and the pattern of the burl is symmetrical on both sides of each joint.

Book-Matching. Turning the veneers so that they are mirror images of each other.

Burls. Growths on the sides of trees that produce beautiful veneer patterns.

Butt. The base of the tree from which the roots spring. Slicing into the butt produces a veneer similar in design to that of a burl.

Crotches. The area of the tree formed by two branches.

Field. The central figure of a veneered panel.

Oyster Shell. A decorative veneer pattern produced by slicing the log perpendicular to its length.

Plain-slicing. Slicing through the log as it presents itself.

Quartered Figure. Slicing a log perpendicular to the medullary rays.

Rift. Slicing through a log *almost* perpendicular to the medullary rays.

Rotary-Slicing. The process of mounting the log on a lathe and slowly advancing the knife as the log turns. This quick, inexpensive technique produces very wide slices of veneer with a very bold pattern that are extensively used in plywood.

Slip Match. A veneer pattern created by laying up a panel by slipping several veneer cuts with the same presentation from the top of the stack.

---

the word "veneer" became synonymous with "cheap" and "inferior."

Unfortunately, this stigma from the war years has continued through several generations to the present day. It has been reinforced by experiences with water damage, veneer's chief enemy. It's true that a veneered tabletop will not survive under a soggy potted plant. Even if the veneer survives, substrate materials such as particleboard and MDF (medium-density fiberboard) will swell to a point where the piece becomes irreparable. Too often people will not acknowledge their abuse of a product; it's far easier to blame the product. Few, if any, ever contemplate the damage that would result to solid wood under that same soggy plant.

REASONS FOR USING VENEER

The reasons for using veneer rather than solid wood are many and varied. Economy immediately comes to mind. If you have ever used oak, walnut, or mahogany plywood in a project, the savings become obvious. The cost of the plywood might be almost the same per square foot as solid lumber, but there is no edge gluing and sanding involved, so you save time, and therefore money, on the project. This savings becomes even more obvious when dealing with exotic species, wherein the scarcity of solid wood and the cost of handling and transportation become major factors. And there is also the conservation factor. A rare tree sliced into veneer can adorn many more projects than it could if cut into lumber.

Economy is not the only reason for using veneer. Some designs are impractical in solid wood. Take the example of a coffee table built out of diamond-shaped sections of solid oak. Eventually, through seasonal changes, openings will appear at the center where the points of the diamonds met.

Effects can be achieved with veneer that are virtually impossible with solid wood. A piece of veneer wrapped in spiral fashion about a column lends a dramatic and unique effect to cabinetry or interior finish. (This is described in Chapter 6.) Veneer placed cross-grain in one character of a molding produces an effect that the eye doesn't expect. (This is also described in Chapter 6.) Veneer is often used in Mission-style furniture to display the quartered figure of oak on all four sides of large components—an effect impossible in solid wood without four-piece construction.

Curved surfaces take on a far different and more pleasing look when veneered. The grain of veneer is smooth, flowing, and of even color and texture, while the grain of the wood beneath the veneer changes from end grain to flat grain, often varying in texture. Here, too, cost plays a factor, for the waste encountered in building anything curved is easier to tolerate in an economical species covered with exotic veneer than it would be in the exotic species of solid wood.

Some wood is not suitable for lumber. Satinwood comes immediately to mind. Though satinwood makes a beautiful veneer, lumber cut from this species checks—both across and through the grain. Zebrawood has similar characteristics. And imagine the complications involved in making a raised door

panel out of a board cut from a crotch or a burl. The instability and poor machining characteristics of these types of woods are frightening.

HOW VENEER IS CUT

Thin slices of wood can be taken from a log by sawing, splitting, riving, or slicing. Most likely, in days of old all these techniques were used. Today, however, most veneer is sliced with a huge knife. That knife can be as long as 17 feet, although it's rare to see slices longer than 12 feet—more often six to eight feet. In many species, it's hard to find a much longer log that's worth slicing.

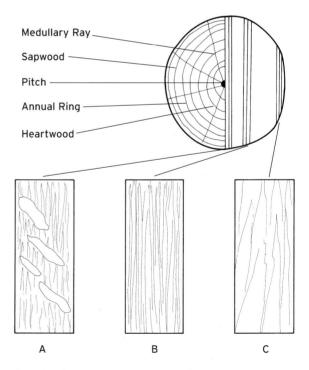

1-2. Plain-sliced veneer. C shows the first slices produced. B shows a rift figure that is produced as cutting continues. A shows a quartered figure.

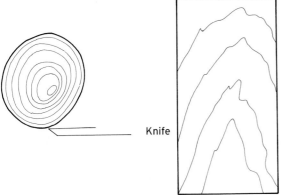

1-3. Rotary-sliced veneer.

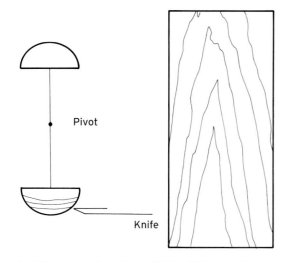

1-4. Veneer produced by a slightly different rotary manner than that shown in **1-3.**

Preparatory to slicing, the logs are checked with a metal detector. Nails, pieces of wire, and other metal can damage the expensive and difficult-to-sharpen knife. The logs are "barked" (that is, bark is removed from them), and to accommodate the machinery they may be halved or quartered. They may also be squared up with a saw, providing some lumber from the outer edges, or at least eliminating the need to trim the veneers to manageable sizes and shapes. The logs—or timbers—are then soaked in hot water or exposed to steam for as long as it takes to

soften them; often, days are involved in the heating process.

After the log is prepared, it may be taken to different types of slicing machines. *Plain-slicing* is shown in **1–2.** The first few slices produce a figure like that shown in C of the drawing. As the slicing progresses, a different figure will appear called *rift* (B). And as the knife nears the center of the log, cutting parallel with the medullar rays, a *quartered figure* appears (A).

The log may also be mounted on a lathe and the knife slowly advanced as it is turned, as shown in **1–3.** This technique produces some very wide slices of veneer with a very bold character. These *rotary-sliced veneers* are extensively used in plywood, for the process is quick and inexpensive. But some types of veneer can only be achieved by rotary slicing; bird's-eye maple comes immediately to mind.

Logs may also be mounted on a slightly different rotary machine and sliced, as shown in **1–4.** Slices produced by this technique are wider than those produced by plain-slicing, and will have a character bolder than plain-sliced veneer but not nearly as bold as rotary-sliced veneer.

If the log—more often smaller limbs—is sliced perpendicular to its length, a decorative figure called "oyster shell" is produced (**1–5**). This particular figure can be most

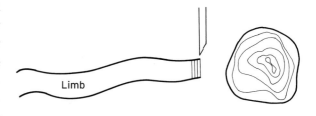

1-5. Oyster-shell figure.

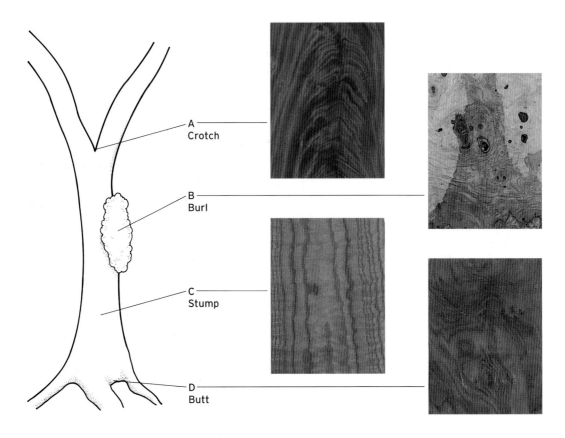

1-6. Veneers produced by slicing various parts of a tree.

dramatic if it is sliced from deformed, non-symmetrical limbs.

Parts of a tree other than the main trunk and larger limbs can be sliced to produce veneer, and this can result in very dramatic, decorative figures, as shown in 1–6. Slices taken from the crotches (the area of the tree formed by two branches) not only produce different grain directions, but the compression caused by weight concentrated at this area produces a unique wavy pattern (A in 1–6).

Once sliced, those ugly growths on the sides of trees (the burls) render some of the most beautiful figures imaginable (B in 1–6). A wealth of designs can be found in burls.

And let's not forget the stump. The tremendous weight of the tree compresses the fibers of the wood that is located in the first few feet above the ground. This results in a curly figure (C in 1–6). While slices of stump are not usually more than three feet in length, they can be worked into beautiful designs.

Slicing even farther down into the butt—the base of the tree from which the roots spring—yields a design similar to that produced with burl (D in 1–6).

The foregoing information is somewhat oversimplified, but it should give you some idea of how different figures are derived from different parts of the tree and with various cutting techniques.

CARE AFTER SLICING

After falling from the knife, the individual slices are held flat and sent through drying chambers. At the other end, they are stacked in the order in which they were cut from the log. Keeping the slices in order is extremely important for the purpose of properly presenting and matching grain, as discussed in the following pages. To ensure that you don't loose the order of the slices, mark the end with a couple of pencil lines. And, in the case of burls and crotches, number the slices. Before cutting a slice of veneer—and losing the pencil lines—mark a squiggle line on one edge; on the underside—beneath the squiggle line—mark a series of Xs.

HOW VENEER IS SUPPLIED

Species of veneer ordered from the same supplier can vary in quality. Some shipments will come nicely trimmed, all of consistent widths with edges almost suitable for joints. Other shipments may have slices with the outline of the log; slices that seem rather thick and ragged; or slices that are somewhat thinner and appear to have been sanded.

Mills in various countries have slightly different standards. Some mills are better equipped than others. Also, some species can't be sliced as thin as others. All of these factors contribute to the irregularities.

Even though veneer catalogues say that the veneer is between $1/28$ and $1/32$ inch thick, this often isn't the case. The cedar veneer used for the blanket chest described in Chapter 11 measured $3/32$ inch, was twisted, and was rougher than a corncob, while the Benin veneer used for the dining table described in Chapter 13 was substantially under $1/32$ inch, heavenly flat, and appeared to have been sanded. While the catalogue said that the cedar would be three feet in length, it was actually two feet. And while the catalogue said that the Benin would be "...up to eight feet in length," it actually measured ten feet, six inches.

Burls and crotches vary dramatically, depending on the species of wood and the type of cut. If you have a specific design in mind, always call your supplier and have him check his inventory for the sizes needed. This holds true for vertical-grain material as well as figured cuts.

PAPER-BACKED VENEER

Veneers are also supplied bonded to a paper backing. Usually they are 8 feet in length and 18 inches wide, but widths up to 48 inches are not uncommon. Narrow strips are supplied in long rolls with hot melt glue on the paper; these strips are to be used for facing. Some sheets are even supplied with a peel-and-stick system. Peel-and-stick veneer is expensive.

CROSS-BANDED VENEER

Cross-banded veneer consists of a face veneer bonded to a less expensive species with the grain running perpendicular to the face. There are several companies that supply cross-banded veneers. Some supply veneers bonded to a plastic-laminate backing sheet. Essentially, you're buying a two-ply piece of plywood. You specify the size and design and the company does all of the cutting, fitting, and patching of the veneer where necessary. These folks do charge for their work, but they can help you produce a magnificent tabletop or some elegant door panels with minimum effort on your part.

VENEER PRESENTATIONS

There are four different ways to show or present the face side of a slice of veneer, as shown in **1–7**. These can be demonstrated by considering one single fiber of wood in a slice of veneer. This fiber lies in the slice not quite parallel to the edges—a highly likely situation, as shown in **1–7**. If the slice were to be turned over, the fiber would appear as B in **1–7**. Turning it end for end would result in C. And turning B end for end produces D. To prevent confusing these four different slices of veneer, make a squiggle line on one side of the slice and the Xs under it.

So, why should you be aware of veneer presentation? In many species, this is very important. Wood possesses iridescent properties; that is, it produces lustrous rainbow-like colors that result from light reflection. In some hardwood species this can be very dramatic, and is referred to as the "depth" or "fire" in the wood. The same characteristic is found in softwood species but is not always as dramatic.

Look at **1–7** and observe the lines that represent light coming from a single source. The reflected light in A and D is similar, but not identical. Likewise in B and C. Observe how dramatically the reflection differs between A and B or A and C. Are you beginning to see the color possibilities?

Now, if you were to lay up a panel by slipping several veneer cuts with the same presentation from the top of the stack—creating a "slip match"—the light reflections from all cuts would be the same. This is shown in **1–8**. The joints would not be obvious, except for grain-match challenges. With this type of match, the cuts can be slipped back and forth to accommodate the grain, but the method is wasteful (A in **1–8**).

If you were to "book-match" the veneers—that is, turn the cuts as if turning the pages of a book or laying out the pleats of an accordion so that they are mirror images of each other, as shown in **1–9**—the presentation of each would produce opposite light reflections. This type of matching certainly overcomes the grain-matching challenges, but while walking around the panel, you will find that in one position one cut looks light and the next dark. The joints will stand out as the straight lines they are. The finishing process makes the difference even more dramatic.

If you were to lay up a diamond-design tabletop as shown in **1–10**, as you walk around the top at one point one diamond shape would look light and the opposite one

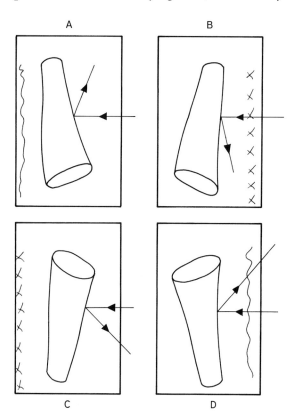

1-7. The light that reflects on a veneer depends on how the veneer is presented.

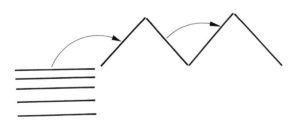

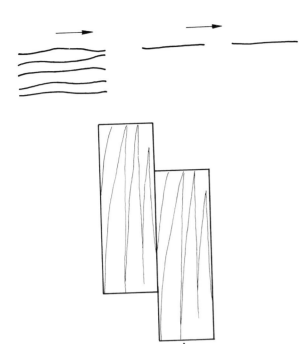

1-8. A "slip-match" effect.

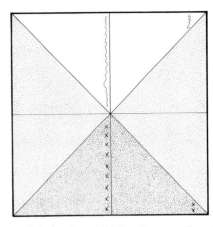

1-10. Diamond design for a tabletop. Compare the effect of this design to that in **1-11**.

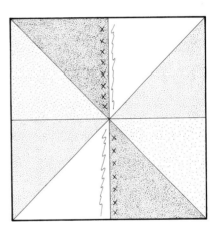

1-11.

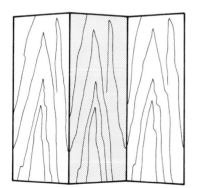

1-9. Book-matched veneer.

dark. The other two would fall somewhere in between. Laying up the veneers as shown in **1–11** would produce a different effect. Here the opposite quadrants of the diamond shapes would reflect light differently.

Burls work the same way. If two slices of a stack of four burl slices were to be flipped, as shown in **1–12**, and then the top ones turned end for end, the result would be a "book and butt" match. In this case, the same corner of each slice would touch in the center, and the pattern of the burl would be symmet-

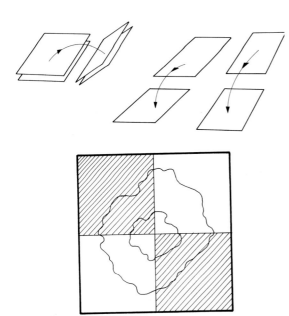

1-12. Burls with a "book and butt match."

rical on both sides of each joint. And what about the light? Well, it would reflect the same in opposite quadrants.

It should be emphasized that simply laying up veneers in any random manner can be devastating, but with a little care and planning the effects of light reflection can produce some interesting and beautiful results.

SPECIES CHARACTERISTICS

While many veneers are very similar, some have their own characteristics that will pose challenges. Giving proper attention to these quirks can save a world of troubleshooting and repairs. Below is a description of some of these characteristics and ways to deal with them.

Oils and Resins

Some woods are very resinous. Teak, satinwood, and some rosewoods are particularly troublesome. These veneers can contain so much oils and resin that glue will not stick to them. The degree to which they will repel glue depends on the particular log from which they were sliced. It can get so bad that bonding these veneers is like bonding a piece of waxed paper. And when contact cement is used, the oils will mix with the glue and prevent it from drying, leaving a gooey mess on the surface.

Softwood species such as pine contain pitch around knots that will inhibit the effect of adhesives.

Pitch, resins, and oils can also pose a challenge in finishing because they can bleed through to the surface or inhibit drying. Solvent-based finishes such as varnish, lacquer, and Danish oil will either not dry or dry very slowly on surfaces with these materials. Water-based finishes will dry, but they will float and peel easily. Wax will never harden or, if it does, it will take months. Catalyzed resin finishes won't harden on some species and will remain soft.

Solution? Before working with these veneers, scrub with a strong solvent such as acetone or lacquer thinner. Don't just wipe off the surface; get out a brush and scrub. Some craftsmen even recommend soaking the veneers in solvent. Soaking would be particularly important when bonding the veneer with contact cement. Any oils in the wood will eventually find their way into the glue line, severely weakening it.

End Checks, Splits, and Tears

Rough handling often causes tears or splits along the grain (**1–13**). To prevent these from getting worse, tape them immediately (The use of veneer tape is discussed thoroughly in Chapter 3.)

Checks pose a different challenge. They

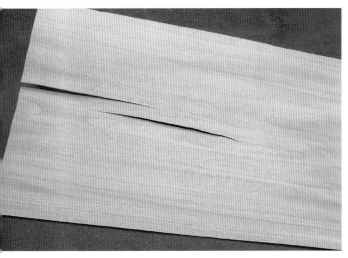

1-13. Splits from rough handling.

appear as a V-shaped void in the end of the cut—a void that may have been in the log from which the veneer was sliced. If the void is less than a quarter inch in width, it is possible to pull the check together and tape it. This will, of course, cause the end of the veneer to cup or bow, depending on which side you are looking at. The stress caused by the cup will have to be relieved. Sometimes this can be done successfully, and sometimes not.

The quickest way to flatten out that cup is to spray the area with a fine mist of water; try to avoid spraying the tape because water will loosen it. Then, with an iron set on medium heat, slowly iron the veneer flat, turning the veneer frequently. Continue until the veneer is dry. If you have met with only moderate success, spray and iron once more.

Another thing to consider is any stain on the sides of the check. These often come from the log and can be permanent. Try sanding or scraping to see if the stain is only on the surface. If the stain is well set, a V-shaped section of the veneer will have to be cut out and a patch of similar grain taped in. (Patching is discussed on pages 120 and 121.) By all means,

however, if you can do without that checked end, cut it off and throw it away.

No, don't save that checked end for the project you're thinking of building. Little pieces of veneer can grow into piles, taking up valuable space, to say nothing of the fire hazard. Keep a few of these end cuts for borders or experiments, but dispose of the rest. Give these pieces to a friend who is working on a marquetry mural.

Thin and Thick Areas and Grain Holes

Veneers sliced parallel with the medullar rays of the log often contain thin spots. Quartered oak and lacewood come to mind as being major offenders. In these species, the thin spots are in the figure resulting from the ray. Holding the veneer up to a strong light will reveal areas that are unusable. Cutting through a thin spot, you'll find that the veneer is only a couple thousandths of an inch thick.

Holding veneer to the light will also reveal coarse, grainy areas that are certain to allow the glue to bleed through. Should these be encountered, think carefully about the glue you intend to use and the manner in which the veneer will be bonded to the substrate. (Refer to Chapter 5 for information on these subjects.) Always be sure to use a cover of heavy paper or plastic if you're using a press. This will prevent the work from sticking to the press components. Also consider whether your finishing technique will be afftected by bleed-through.

Thick areas will usually be found in defects such as knots. This is because the veneer has shrunk more than the knot. Compression bands running through stump wood and crotches will often be a little thicker than the surrounding wood. Here, again, uneven shrinkage is the cause.

It veneers with thin and thick areas are

bonded with a press, thick areas may be starved for glue while the thin areas can have an overly thick glue line. These challenges are not insurmountable. They are discussed in Chapter 5.

Mineral Deposits

As a tree grows, it pulls water, and, consequently, dissolved minerals from the ground. In many species, this results only in a unique coloration of the wood. Some deposits are more dramatic. Those dark lines running through some slices of teak are mineral deposits, and they are very hard. Brazilian rosewood and Koa also contain mineral deposits.

If a cabinet scraper is pulled over some mineral deposits, the deposits often put nicks in the burr of the scraper. And hand-sanding with soft sandpaper will leave the deposits proud or higher than the surrounding wood—to say nothing of dulling the sandpaper quickly. Mineral deposits can leave dull spots in router cutters that are used for trimming—even carbide cutters.

Color Retention

Almost all wood species, especially when exposed to the sun's ultraviolet rays, change color to some extent. For example, walnut fades from purple to warm brown, mahogany and cherry darken, oak yellows, and the green in poplar turns brown very quickly. The point is: If you have a specific color scheme in mind, be sure the woods will maintain that color scheme in the years to come or make sure the pieces will never be exposed to UV (ultraviolet) light. Keeping the pieces out of UV light may sound impossible, but many new homes are being built incorporating UV-resistant glass windows.

To understand how veneer color can

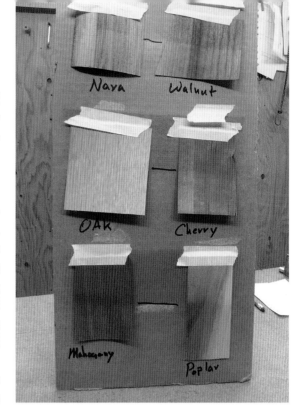

1-14. Demonstration of sun fade.

change, take a small piece of the veneer you intend to use and tape a piece of cardboard or heavy paper over half of it. Leave it in the sun for a week or two. You may be very surprised when you remove the cardboard.

The veneer samples shown in **1–14** spent only two weeks in a south window in March. The change in the walnut, nara, and poplar veneer is rather dramatic. If you are considering using poplar for its green and white colors, don't. Note that the green turns warm brown and the white yellows. The red oak has yellowed some, and this gets more dramatic with further exposure. The mahogany lightened, and this too increases. The cherry was somewhat of a disappointment. In lumber, it usually darkens.

Holes

Some figured species and burls in particular can be riddled with holes. Olive ash will have holes where knot-like defects have fallen out during handling. Carpathian elm will have voids where no wood was formed in the growth process. If these holes are small, they can be patched with wood putty, but larger holes must be filled with a patch cut from a similar piece of veneer. (Refer to pages 120 and 121 for information on patching.)

Worms and insects also leave behind evidence of their passing. If wormholes can be cut out in fitting and preparation, it is best to do so. Small wormholes in inconspicuous places can also be filled with putty and touched up in the finishing process.

Wrinkles

Raw veneer is not always supplied in a perfectly flat condition. You may not realize just how wrinkled some slices are until you begin working with them. Figured species are usually distorted in all directions.

Surface Compression and Checking

As a piece of veneer is sliced, it is forced to curl away from the parent log and the slicing knife—much the same as a shaving leaves a hand plane. This causes the side nearer the log to stretch, while the side away from it is forced to compress. It is almost impossible in some species to detect which side is which; in other species, the effects are dramatic to the point of defect. The log side can be stretched to the point of checking, and the other compressed to a point that it will repel glue or finishing products.

Fortunately, slicing defect is easy to spot. Gently bend the veneer along the grain in both directions. You will notice that there is resistance in one direction, while the veneer yields easily in the other (1–15). If the compressed side is up, the veneer will bend upward easily. You could wrap it around a soda can. If the stretched side is up, the veneer will not be as yielding and cracking sounds will often be heard.

Another method is to examine the veneer under magnification—a photographer's 8x loupe works well. The compressed side will be tight, often to the extent of being shiny. The stretched side will show tiny checks as it is bent away from the loupe.

In application, the compressed side should be up and the stretched side down, allowing the glue to firmly grasp the checks. After bonding, the compressed side should be sanded heavily to break any glaze that exists, permitting the acceptance of stain and other finishing products.

Book-matching cuts with slicing defects poses a challenge, but it is by no means insurmountable. Scuff the compressed side with coarse sandpaper so it will accept glue properly. And after bonding, sand heavily to the approximate center of the veneer in order to remove the checks. Only you will notice any defect that remains.

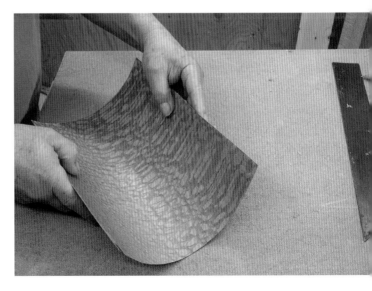

1-15. Veneer bends well in one direction while resisting in the other.

Characteristics of Paper-Backed and Cross-Banded Veneers

There are advantages and disadvantages to using paper-backed and cross-banded veneers. These veneers do not contain oils, checks, splits, holes, etc. The manufacturer has already dealt with these problems. Also, the glue line between the paper and the wood, coupled with the glazed surface of the paper, inhibits the rapid absorption of glue solvents, be the solvent water or petroleum. In the case of water, this limits the expansion of the veneer, reducing pulling and open joints, which are investigated in Chapter 5. In the case of contact cement, the glaze reduces the number of coats needed for bonding.

Another advantage is that the paper backing strengthens veneer dramatically. Those delicate burls that will disintegrate easily can be handled as roughly as needed. Vertical-grain species can be handled without fear of cracking. And, both may be cut and fit with little more care than would be given the paper itself.

Now for the disadvantages: Paper-backed veneers are often very thin—at least the wood component is thin. Sanding should be done with extreme care. In some instances, the wood is so thin that the paper and glue can be seen through it. The glue seals the veneer in places, and when a penetrating stain is used, these areas produce blotchy colors.

Also, paper-backed veneers can vary in thickness from species to species, and even more drastically from manufacturer to manufacturer. This difference in thickness is not as drastic as it was years ago, when the product was first introduced, but it does still exist. Use caution when doing decorative work with a number of different paper-backed veneers, and check all that will be used for consistent thickness.

The glaze on backing paper can cause beading of water-based adhesives. This can be a nuisance when using glues that have been thinned, as in the dry-glue process discussed on pages 91 to 95. It is not an insurmountable challenge. Simply break the glaze using 80-grit sandpaper.

Paper-backed veneers are very attractive—often, too attractive. If you've ever wondered why you can't buy lumber as good-looking as veneer, it's because veneer mills are prepared to pay premium prices for choice logs, so these logs never make it to board form. This attractiveness can get to the point where the veneer looks phony, such as when it resembles plastic laminate.

Suppliers usually roll paper-backed veneers for shipment. Some try to pack each shipment into the smallest possible container. Paper-backed veneers treated thus have a tendency to stay rolled up, or at least the curve seems permanent. If you come across such veneer, roll the veneer loosely in the opposite direction and let it stand for an hour or two. In most cases, the veneer will once again become flat. If not, roll it tighter and let stand longer.

If you intend to work with paper-backed veneer exclusively, you will be limited to the few species available. Oh yes, some paper-backed suppliers have a rather impressive list of species, but it is nowhere as large as the lists provided by suppliers of raw veneer.

Paper-backed veneers generally cost more per square foot than raw veneers. While they come in sheets as large as 48 x 96 inches, there will be cutting waste just as with the raw material. And there will be leftovers. These are things to consider when choosing the material for a particular project.

CHAPTER 2

TOOLS AND EQUIPMENT

CUTTING TOOLS

Veneer is not a particularly hard substance and can be easily cut in a variety of ways. The grain direction and fragile nature of some veneers pose a challenge. In this respect, no cutting method, tool, or technique will work in all situations. Below I describe the usefulness of various tools and equipment.

Straightedges

Most of the cuts made in veneer will be straight cuts, and for these you will need some kind of guide. This guide could be anything from a very expensive machined, steel straightedge to a ripping from a sheet of plywood. No matter what type of straightedge is used, there are a couple of important criteria it should meet.

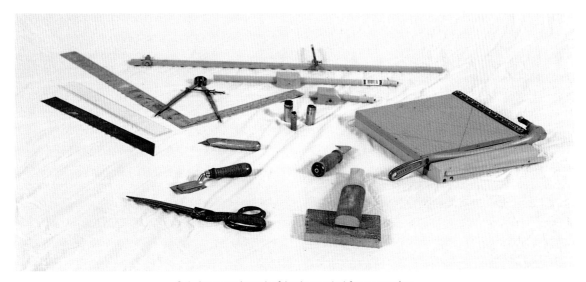

2-1. An assortment of tools needed for veneering.

Here is a suggested list of tools and shop aids that will prove helpful when working with veneer:

For Layout:

A. Trammels

B. Scribing devices (at least two, one for scribing from the edge and one for scribing patterns)

C. 45-degree plastic triangles in different sizes

D. A good straightedge (a carpenter's square will suffice for small projects)

For Cutting Veneer:

A. Veneer saw

B. Rotary or paper cutter (handy to have, but not necessary)

C. Various knives with disposable blades, to be determined by reader based on the type of work they intend to do (see pages 27 and 28 for more information)

D. Linoleum knife

E. A good pair of heavy-duty scissors or tin snips

F. Carving tools, such as gouges (to make curved veneer cuts in a tight radius)

For Bonding Veneer to the Substrate:

A. Veneer punches of various sizes to accommodate the size of holes that need to be patched.

B. Sanding blocks with various grits of sandpaper

C. Glue spreaders

D. Hammer

E. Household iron

F. Clamps (spring clamps and a screw clamp are helpful)

G. Adhesive (see Chapter 5 for a discussion of the various adhesives and their advantages and disadvantages)

It goes without saying that a straightedge must be straight, but it must also be wide enough to be held firmly and safely. Using a narrow straightedge, you will be more prone to hold it by placing your fingertips too near the guiding edge. In these situations, it is possible to trim a long fingernail or shave off a fingertip using a straightedge and knife. Use a straightedge at least two inches wide.

It is also important that the straightedge does not slip, for a slippery straightedge will always spoil that most important cut. One way to prevent straightedges from slipping is to place strips of masking tape on them. Masking tape is thin enough that it doesn't interfere with the straightedge, and the rough surface helps immensely. (Double-faced sticky tape is too sticky and too thick.) The masking tape doesn't stay rough forever, but it can be quickly replaced.

Another way to prevent straightedges from slipping is to drill holes the exact size of a pushpin into them. Then, when making long cuts, or cuts in wrinkled material, tap a pushpin through the holes (2–2). The pin not only holds the straightedge in place, it also prevents any movement of the veneer on the bench top. If using flexible steel straightedges—through which it is impossible to drill a hole—place pins opposite the waste side to prevent the straightedge from drifting into the field (2–3).

Use pushpins with metal heads. Don't use plastic pushpins. When tapped with a hammer or pushed forcefully with the thumb, the plastic breaks and the metal shank winds up in the thumb.

Clear-plastic layout tools can also be used as straightedges for cutting. Some can be equipped with masking tape, and all can have holes for pins. These have the advantage of allowing an unobstructed view of the work.

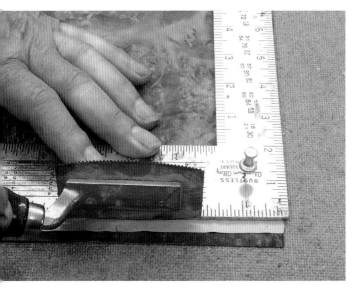

2-2. A pushpin inserted through a hole in a straightedge will prevent movement.

2-4. Pressure on a straightedge beyond the veneer will prevent tearing.

2-3. A pushpin set behind a straightedge will prevent drifting.

See Layout Tools on pages 39 to 41 for more information.

The straightedge does more than provide a guide for the cutting tool; it also supports the veneer. In cutting across grain—or partially across grain—it is important to hold the straightedge down firmly. This prevents the veneer from buckling under the pressure of the cutting tool. When cutting with the grain, keeping firm pressure on the straightedge will help prevent the cutting tool from tearing slivers from the workpiece.

One more thing to consider is that last little bit of cross-grain cut. Keeping firm pressure on the straightedge beyond the veneer will help in preventing the forward pressure of the knife from splitting away that last quarter inch or so (**2–4**).

Knives with Disposable Blades

The mainstay of general shop knives is the utility knife. These are readily available, inexpensive, and have disposable blades. Some even have sectioned blades, the tip of which can be broken off as it becomes dull. These are not good for most veneer work.

The utility knife is fine for making rough cuts, but should not be used when precision is required. The blade flexes too much, so the user does not feel the body of the knife wander when the blade follows the grain. The util-

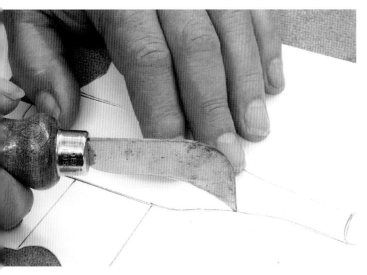

2-5. A floor-covering knife permits clear view of the line being cut.

ity knife does have the advantage that it permits you to vary the angle of attack. This can come in handy when cutting joints where the question of the blade following the grain is not an issue.

Also because of flexing blades, smaller hobby knives with disposable blades are a poor choice. By virtue of the wide assortment of blades available, these knives do have a place in delicate marquetry, and they are recommended highly for that purpose, but they are useless for the heavy-duty work involved in veneering.

One other disposable-blade knife worthy of mention is the hook knife. The workhorse of the floor-covering installer, this knife is also useful in wood veneering. Its blade is similar to the utility-knife blade in size and thickness, but rather than a sharpened edge there is a groove cut in the blade and the edges of the groove are sharpened.

This knife is most useful in making rough cuts—especially rough, curved cuts. While the knife is unpredictable going with the grain, cuts that are partially across grain can be made most successfully. Unfortunately, raw wood veneer does not have the internal strength to withstand the pressures of cuts being made directly across grain.

Hook-knife blades can be found in different sizes. The blade with the smallest groove is best for making straight cuts and curved cuts with a gentle radius. Blades with a wider groove will make tighter cuts, and if you round off the tip of the blade so that it won't scratch, these wide blades are excellent for edge-trimming.

Linoleum Knives

Possibly the most useful tool for cutting veneer is the linoleum knife or floor-covering knife. These have a blade that allows little or no flexing, and the shape of the blade allows clear view of the line being cut or the straight-edge being followed (**2–5**).

The linoleum knife does need periodic sharpening, but it is a minor inconvenience to stop and pass the edge over a sharpening stone and strop. Sharpen only ¼ inch of the tip of the knife. You can even round off the remaining cutting edge, to prevent getting your fingers tangled up with that part. The backside of the knife proves most useful in pressing down veneer tape or firming up a joint.

When cutting with a linoleum knife, do not try to make a cut with one single pass. On the first pass, apply a little more pressure than the weight of the knife itself, while holding the knife firmly against the guiding surface you are using. This is important if the cut being made has a chance of following the grain. With each successive pass, increase the pressure until the veneer is cut through—five passes are often required. Think of the linoleum knife as a saw with one tooth and no set.

Veneer Saws

If you don't have a veneer saw, get one. Cutting long joints with the grain in most species of wood can be done more accurately with a veneer saw than any other tool—save for a shear. A veneer saw seems to hold up better than a knife in cutting abrasive wood species such as teak or rosewood.

Veneer saws do have some set, and as a result don't always make the smoothest cut. This roughness can damage delicate veneers. The set is also devastating to the straightedge or to the saw itself. It either grinds away at the straightedge or, if a hardened-steel straightedge is being used, the saw teeth become worn.

One remedy for the effects of the set is to remove it, that is, to sharpen the saw like a knife. This results in a large number of sharp teeth. The large number of sharp teeth enable a veneer saw to be used far longer between sharpening than the single "tooth" of the linoleum knife or the single tip of a utility knife. This type of veneer saw is most useful when making straight cuts in delicate burls and crotches. Refer to Modifying a Veneer Saw, which follows, for details on sharpening.

Modifying a Veneer Saw

As with general-woodworking saws, you really should have at least two veneer saws—one for ripping and one for crosscutting. (If you have ever tried ripping a board with a crosscut saw—or vice versa—you can appreciate the need for two saws.) However, there really aren't veneer saws designed for ripping. But with a file, a vise, and a belt sander—or sharpening stone—a veneer saw can be modified to make all cuts, rip, crosscuts, and diagonal.

To do this, mount the blade in a vise with a small stick backing it so that the jaws won't flatten the countersink screw holes. Then,

2-6. Grooves have been ground in the tang of a veneer saw to aid in securing it in the handle.

2-7. Reshaping the teeth on a veneer-saw blade.

Shop-Made Veneer Saw

The stainless-steel veneer saw shown in this section can be used when working with hot hide glue. The stainless steel won't leave blue stains on the wet surface of the veneer if left in contact with it for any length of time—as will carbon steel.

For the stainless-steel saw, a serrated table knife can be used. After mounting a knife in the vise, file its teeth, using the knife's serrations as a spacing guide **(2-9)**. The knives may then be sharpened as described under Modifying a Veneer Saw on page 29. These types of knife/saw hold an edge remarkably well.

2-8. A close-up of the blade teeth. Note the reshaped teeth on the right of the blade.

with a triangular needle file reshape the teeth (**2–7** and **2–8**).

Notice the teeth on the left of the blade in **2–8**; these are the shape of the teeth in most veneer saws. They are crosscut teeth, tilting forward. Now notice the few teeth reshaped on the right of the blade. They are shaped like equilateral triangles, tilting in no particular direction. These teeth will rip veneer very well; they will also crosscut very well. In addition, they can be pulled or pushed across the veneer with equal cutting action.

In reshaping the teeth, it's a good practice to keep your thumb on top of the file, feeling the flat area. The cutting angle of the file can then be easily sensed and held in place by the position of the wrist.

To the right of the vise in **2–7** is a loupe. That little magnifier is helpful in determining how good a job you've done. It's always helpful to have some form of magnification handy to critically evaluate any sharpening job.

2-9. Filing the saw teeth for a stainless-steel saw.

Once the teeth are reshaped, the blade should be sharpened like a knife. The object here is to form a bevel of about 15 degrees on only one side of the saw, the side that will be opposite the straight edge. With the saw's blade sharpened thus, the veneer under the straightedge will be prepared for a joint with no need to use a shooting block. Considering the 15-degree cutting angle, even the side of the veneer opposite the straightedge will be ready for a joint with only a pass or two of the shooting block. For the sharpening process a grinder or stone could be used, but a belt sander will work equally as well (2–10). Keep a bucket of water at hand for cooling, as the blade will become quite warm.

It's possible to remove too much metal with the sander, turning pointed teeth into teeth with flat spots on the top. If that happens, return the blade to the vise and reshape any teeth with flat tops. When you are satisfied with your work, pass a slipstone over the side opposite the bevel to remove any burr that might grind away at the straightedge.

Although a bit unconventional, this type of veneer saw takes little or no kerf and requires less effort than a conventional veneer saw. It does require periodic sharpening, but it is very gentle with those delicate veneers.

Rotary Cutters

Rotary cutters are available in fabric and office-supply stores. Provided that the rotary cutter is kept sharp and free of nicks, it is not prone to follow the grain, and a cut can often be made in a single pass. It can even be used on freehand curves with a gentle radius. While rotary cutters work best on paper-backed veneer, they will work to a certain degree on raw veneer.

After leaving the floor-covering store with your new linoleum knife, stop by the office-supply store and buy a rotary cutter. They're both good investments.

2-10. Sharpening the edge of the saw.

Paper Cutters

A paper cutter is a fine tool for cutting small pieces of wood. These are available with a blade as long as 30 inches. A larger shear would be an even better piece of equipment, but only if you are doing a great deal of veneering would the cost be justified.

If using a paper cutter, it might be helpful to put strips of masking tape on its table to keep the veneer from slipping. These are placed about one inch back from the bar to prevent them from interfering with the action of the knife. Also, make a couple of 45-degree marks on the table to help line up miter cuts. If you have a lot of cuts to make at a particular angle, use several strips of masking tape as a fence to hold the veneer in position (**2–11**).

Be careful when using a paper cutter; it can cut fingers. If the piece on the table is quite small, hold it down with a block of wood. Also hesitate about a half-second before pulling that handle to make sure your fingertips are clear of the shear.

2-11. Strips of masking tape on a paper cutter table provide a temporary fence.

Scissors and Snips

Scissors can also be used to cut veneer. Heavy-duty scissors work best, and they should be kept sharp. In lieu of scissors, good-quality tin snips will work. Snips will often cut a tighter radius. If you decide to use snips and/or shears, keep pairs in the workshop to be exclusively for veneer. Do not use them, for example, to cut sandpaper. While they served that purpose nicely, the cutting edge became well rounded in a very short time.

CUTTING SURFACE

In most cutting operations, the cutting edge, or tip, of the cutting instrument will pass through the veneer and come into contact with the surface that supports the veneer. In order to keep instruments sharp, try to choose a surface that won't dull the cutting instrument. One possibility is to use the substrate—a few fine knife or saw marks won't hurt it. There are times when hardboard will be useful. The backside of vinyl floor covering is good because it's not slippery. Cardboard will work, but it is spongy and falls apart quickly. Particleboard can also be used, but it is just rough enough to deflect a knife, causing the cuts to become ragged. Another possibility is battleship linoleum, a very durable material that is expensive and somewhat difficult to find.

CARVING TOOLS

When working with inlays and borders, it is often necessary to make curved cuts with a tight radius. Wood-carving tools will accomplish this task with little challenge.

Carving tools can split the veneer near the cut. To eliminate this possibility, make a

2-12. Woodcarving tools may be used to cut curves. Digging the tool in one corner and rolling its edge over the line to be cut eliminates the possibility of damage to the surrounding wood.

rough cut using a hook knife and then trim to the line using the carving tool. The tool can be tapped with a mallet, but digging in one corner and rolling the tool's edge over the line to be cut eliminates the possibility of damage to the surrounding wood (**2–12**). This technique will also permit you to use carving tools with a sweep that doesn't quite match the radius being cut.

You will also find carving gouges very handy for punching round holes (**2–13**). Here again dig in one corner, but then twist the tool. The cutting edge will follow itself if the sweep is true.

POWER TOOLS

Although power tools are obviously used extensively in general woodworking, they are not needed to cut and fit veneer—with the exception of the scroll saw, which is used for marquetry work. See Chapter 8 for more information on scroll saws.

Some power sanding equipment has merit, and this will be discussed as we progress.

PUNCHES

As discussed, burls are ugly growths in the sides of a tree, but they yield such beautiful figured veneers. When these are sliced and the slices dried, defects often fall away, leaving holes in the veneer. These holes need to be patched. A quick and accepted method of patching these holes calls for a "veneer punch." Available in several sizes, this tool punches out an irregularly shaped hole that contains any defect that cannot be worked with. The same tool is then used to punch a patch of similar grain and color from another piece of burl.

A round punch could be used for this purpose, but the irregular shape of the veneer punch makes a less noticeable patch than a perfect circle.

2-13. Woodcarving gouges may be used as punches.

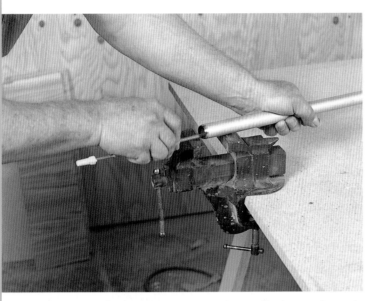

2-14. Making a veneer punch. Here the burr on the end of a piece of electrical conduit is being cleaned.

2-16. Flattening the cutting edge with a file.

2-15. Squeezing the conduit into an irregular shape.

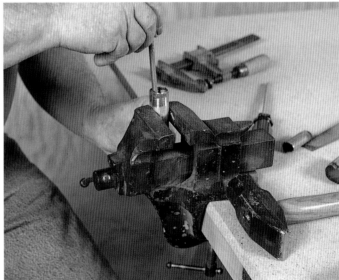

2-17. Deburring the inside of the conduit with a rat-tail file.

Patching Technique

When patching a piece of veneer, don't go after every tiny hole. Most defects will be areas of knots, and small holes can be filled with putty and colored in the finishing operation. Attend to any defect over ½ inch. Before any punching, tape the area to be worked; this will prevent you from doing more damage to the area you

Shop-Made Punches

Veneer punches are costly considering the amount of punching you might do. Making your own will save money. Here's one way: Start by grinding a sharp edge in the end of a piece of thin-wall electrical conduit. Then clean the burr from the inside with a rat-tail file **(2-14)**. Sometimes this takes several trips from file to grinder and back to form a sharp edge of about 30 degrees.

After sharpening, cut about 2¹/₂ inches from the prepared end of the conduit and put it in a vise in order to squeeze it into a slight oval. Then with a clamp, screwdriver, or what have you begin squeezing it into an irregular shape **(2-15)**. You might even wish to bring a hammer into play.

When you're satisfied with the shape, pass a file lightly over the cutting edge to make sure that it is still flat, again deburring the inside with a rat-tail file **(2-16** and **2-17)**.

Using several different sizes of conduit, you can produce a number of punches that will serve you well **(2-18)**. Of course, they don't have the spring that ejects the punched veneer as a store-bought punch does, but you can push it out using the eraser end of a pencil. These shop-made punches are not as intricate in shape as the store-bought types, but the shape they punch is nowhere as fragile as that of the store-bought variety.

are working on. Sometimes perforated tape on the back side of the veneer works (**2–19**), and sometimes it is better to use a stronger solid tape on the face (**2–20**).

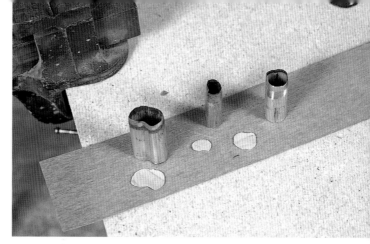

2-18. Shop-made punches.

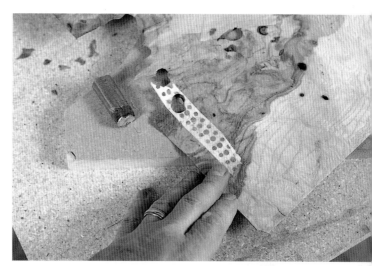

2-19 and 2-20. Patching veneer. Here perforated tape is being used on the veneer back.

2-20. Using solid tape on the face of the veneer.

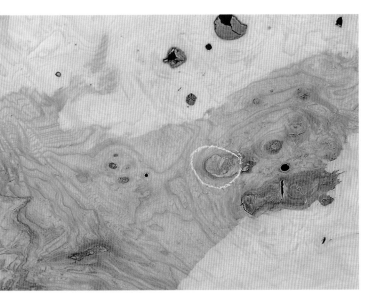

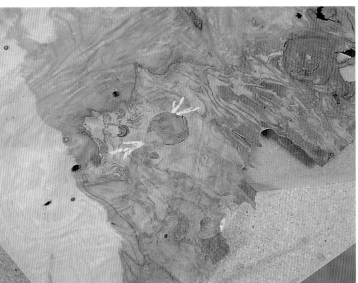

2-21 and 2-22. A close-up of veneer patches.

Casual observers won't spot the patches unless they are looking closely (**2–21** and **2–22**).

HOUSEHOLD IRON

An iron is an indispensable tool that can be used for taping and flattening veneer, and also for a "dry glue" bonding process (see pages 91

to 95). Purchased from a thrift store, an iron is quite economical. You might wish to have more than one for different operations. Here's how to slightly modify one so that it will fit into inside curves: First disassemble it to locate the heating element (**2–23**). Then round off the tip and part of the edges— shown as the shiny areas in **2–24**. (If all you're

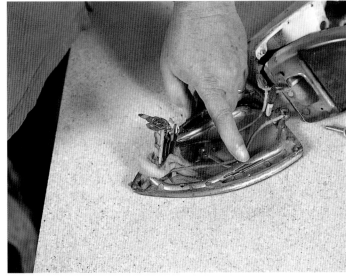

2-23. Modifying a household iron to be used on veneers. Here it is disassembled and the heating element located.

2-24. The shiny areas indicate the tip and edges that have been rounded off.

able to find is a steam iron, be careful to avoid the steam jets.) Round the edges with a disc sander or a file. Make sure that the rounded area is sanded smooth so that it won't damage the veneer.

GLUE CONTAINERS WITH SPREADERS

Cleaning glue-spreading tools after a project can be time-consuming. One way to avoid this step with white and yellow glue is to use a plastic container, such as those containers used for lettuce (2–25). In the container keep a 4-inch paint roller with the handle shortened. Keep about $1/2$ inch of glue at the bottom of the container. Left for a week or two, the glue does deteriorate somewhat, but it's possible to use the glue continually for edge gluing as well as for spreading veneer.

To the right in 2–25 is a clean gallon can that was bought at the local paint store. In the can is a brush. By leaving the brush in the can you won't have to clean it, and it will stay fresh. The bottom of the can contains no more than a half-quart of contact cement. The contact cement is replenished from a gallon or a five-gallon container.

TOOTHED SPREADERS

If you are using a press, you will want some type of toothed spreader for spreading glue. You could of course buy a spreader such as the red trowel-shaped item in 2–26. It has $1/8$-inch teeth, lays down a lot of glue, and is about as coarse as you will ever want to use. To spread less glue, tip the trowel to a 45-degree angle.

You can also make your own spreader. For small projects, you can use a plastic lami-

2-25. Glue container with spreaders.

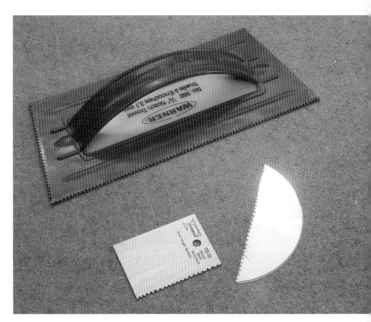

2-26. Toothed spreaders are used for evenly spreading glue.

nate sample in which you have filed notches. For larger projects, a piece of plastic cut from a CD works well.

The wonderful thing about the trowel is the ridges it leaves. When pressure is applied, fresh glue is squeezed from the ridges.

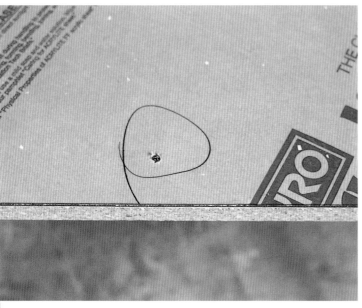

2-27 to 2-29. Cutting plastic sheets. Shown here is a close-up of the rough-cut plastic sheet fastened to a workbench.

2-29. Trimming the plastic sheet with the whole sheet attached to the workbench.

2-28. Trimming the plastic sheet with a router and flush-trim bit.

2-30. Scribing lines on a layout tool.

LAYOUT TOOLS

See-through layout tools and straightedges are very handy for veneer work. When trying to match figure and grain patterns, it is very helpful to have different sizes of transparent marking tools.

Just as with drawing-board layout tools, have at hand different sizes of 45-degree triangles, some 30/60-degree triangles, and a couple of different isosceles triangles with 22½-degree angles if you do a lot of work with octagons. In addition, have an assortment of different lengths of straightedges in assorted widths—2, 2¼, 2½ inches, etc. These will prove handy for laying out and cutting borders.

You can make see-through tools from ⅛- or ¼-inch-thick acrylic or polycarbonate sheet. Polycarbonate sheet is by far stronger. Both types of plastic sheet may be cut on the table saw using a carbide blade. *However, this is dangerous because the plastic often overheats and binds, causing a kickback.* It is far safer to rough-cut the plastic on a band saw and then fasten it to a bench with a straight, smooth edge using a few flathead screws (**2–27**). Then trim it to final dimension with a router and flush-trim bit with the pilot riding on the edge of the bench (**2–28**). Sometimes it's just as easy to screw the whole sheet to the bench and cut it with the router (**2–29**).

Drill holes in all your plastic layout tools to accept a pushpin. This prevents them from wandering. If you want extra lines on your layout triangles so you can use them as a protractor of sorts, you can easily scribe them with a knife or the point of a pair of dividers (**2–30**). The scribed line soon fills with dirt, making it easily visible.

Scribing Dividers

If you do a lot of fitting by scribing, a good pair of dividers is a must. The most important criteria for scribing dividers is that they have a hardened steel needle that can be either sharpened or replaced. To the right in **2–31** is a pair of dividers designed for drafting. There are two problems with these. First, when using them there is the tendency to move the adjustment wheel unknowingly. Second, in tight spots, the body of the instrument gets in the way of the scribing. But they do have replaceable needles and they work in most applications.

To the left in **2–31** is a pair of modified dividers. These are nothing more than an inexpensive pair on which a machinist ground off the tips and bored holes to receive the needles. You can buy the needles at either a drafting-equipment supply store or a supplier that sells tools to floor-covering mechanics. With

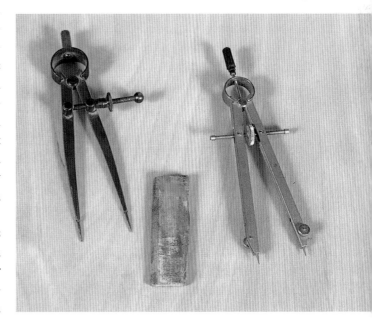

2-31. Scribing dividers.

one drop of CA (cyanoacrylate) adhesive, the needles stay in place until they are heated and pulled out for replacement.

Caution! When heating a needle that has been set in CA, keep in mind that there might be an accumulation of the dried CA at the bottom of the bore. This can boil due to the heat and shoot the needle from the leg of the dividers. Point it in a safe direction.

Also shown in **2–31** is a slip stone; keep it with the dividers to sharpen the point.

Edge Scribes

Two helpful edge scribes are shown in **2–32**. The one at the top is shop-made. The scribing "needle" is a piece of ⅛-inch drill rod that has had its end ground to one side at about a 20-degree angle. It is locked in place by a drywall screw driven into the end of a ⅝-inch dowel. (Run the screw in to establish the threads, withdraw it, and grind off the sharp point to keep it from marring the drill rod.)

The body of the scribe is a simple block of wood drilled to receive the dowel; another drywall screw—with the tip ground off—locks it in place. Note that the front of the body is tapered to allow it to correctly follow tight, inside curves.

Below the shop-made scribe is a needle scribe used by floor-covering mechanics to scribe joints. The joint hook has been pulled off to give it a deeper reach in order to scribe the border for items such as the kidney-shaped desk described in Chapter 12.

When used carefully, both scribes will cut veneer as well as scribe a line. If they don't cut completely through, they will establish a line that is easy to follow with a knife.

Circle Devices

Shown in **2–33** are circle devices. On top is another made in the shop; it is similar to the edge scribe described above. Here the bored block that slides along the dowel has a #3 finishing nail driven into it; the head of the nail is clipped off and the remainder filed to a sharp point. If you intend to cut with such a device, substitute a piece of drill rod for

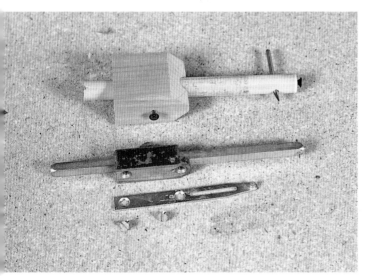

2-32. Edge scribes.

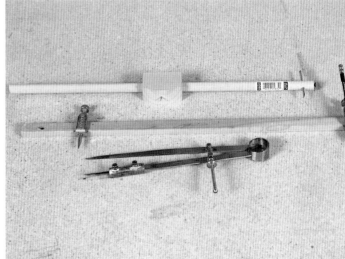

2-33. Circle devices.

the nail as explained for the edge scribe on page 42.

Beneath that is a pair of store-bought trammel points. The beam for the points can be of any length that is convenient. And that pencil can be replaced with a hobby knife or a scribing point.

At the bottom of **2–33** is a simple pair of 8-inch dividers. Slid over one leg is a piece of $1/2$-inch copper pipe. The pipe is slightly squashed to form an oval, and two brass nuts are soldered to it to receive the two stainless-steel locking screws. To solder those nuts on, drill the pipe and insert the screws with the nuts threaded on. You will find that the solder sticks well to the brass nuts and copper pipe, but it doesn't stick to the stainless-steel screws, which will keep the solder from the nut's threads.

2-34. Shop-made veneer hammers.

VENEER HAMMERS

The shop-made veneer hammer shown at the top of **2–34** is nothing more than a handle turned from $13/4$-inch-square stock. Fixed in the end of the handle is a brick chisel. If making this hammer, bore the hole in the handle slightly undersized for the chisel's octagonal shank. After rounding off the cutting edge and corners of the chisel, press it into the bore after swabbing it with hot hide glue.

Below that hammer in **2–34** rests another veneer hammer made on the lathe. In the working head, cut a slot and insert a small piece of $1/4$-inch polycarbonate sheet. Round off its edges and corners and hold it in place with CA adhesive. The plastic-edged contrivance has the advantage that it does not leave a blue stain if left sitting on a piece of wet veneer.

If you live in a cold climate, you probably have an ice scraper in your car. This too

2-35. An assortment of shop-made abrasive devices.

will work for small projects. Just be sure that it has no nicks and round off the corners with sandpaper so that it won't cut into the veneer.

Any of the hammers described here are a must for hot hide glue, but they also work well for putting down contact-cement-bonded veneers.

2-36. An assortment of clamps and weights that includes spring and deep-reach screw clamps, steel plates, and an ingot.

ABRASIVE DEVICES

An abrasive device can be as simple as sandpaper glued to a stick. Keep a large number of such devices scattered all over your shop (2–35). Some are simple, flat blocks that are used for a process called "shooting," which we'll discuss a bit further on. Some have varied radiuses; others are wedge-shaped. Some have crudely formed handles, and others are simply pieces pulled out of the scrap barrel. In all cases, bond industrial-grade sanding cloth— usually 80 grit—to them with contact cement. (Many companies that manufacture sanding belts sell their remnants by the pound.)

Bond the first piece of sandpaper tightly to the stick. When it's time for a replacement, bond a new piece over the first. This one doesn't stick too well, so when it's time to replace it, it's easy to peel off.

You'll see these abrasive devices used often in the following pages; the flat ones are used for shooting straight joints, and the curved ones for shooting curved joints. Both can be used for final trimming.

CLAMPS AND OTHER EQUIPMENT

When working with contact cement, dry glue, or hide glue you are bound to have a spot or two in a piece of veneer that need a little clamping or a weight to hold them for a time (2–36). Spring clamps work great around the edges. Out in the field, sometimes a weight will work. Shown in 2–36 are two pieces of square steel plate and a piece of babbitt ingot that work. A deep-reach screw clamp is always handy, and if it won't reach far enough, it's a simple matter to fasten some extensions with a few drywall screws as shown in the upper part of 2–36. If all else fails, you can span the surface with a stick, put a block under it over the offending spot, and clamp both ends (this is shown in the foreground of 2–36).

No matter what, make sure to keep on hand some paper to place beneath the weight or clamping device to prevent any glue from sticking to the weight or clamps. Also have available a few handy blocks of wood to prevent the clamps from marring the veneer.

CHAPTER 3

PREPARING AND CUTTING VENEER

Veneering consists of several steps: Preparing the veneer for use; laying out and cutting the veneer to the needed dimensions; preparing the substrate for which to bond the veneer; mixing the glue to the proper consistency when necessary; and bonding the veneer and the substrate. This chapter discusses the preparation and cutting of veneer.

PREPARATION

Right from the unpacking of the shipment, veneer does need some care. Should you unpack a shipment and discover damage, first mark one end on the face side (**3–1**). This way, you'll have a reference for proper presentation. Then repair all damage using perforated

3-1. Marking one end of the face side of veneer.

3-2. Repairing damages to veneer using perforated tape.

3-3. Taping the end of veneer with brown paper tape to help locate the face and end.

tape (**3–2**)—just in case the tape winds up in the glue line.

If the veneer is not damaged, tape the ends to prevent the veneer from getting damaged through rough handling in the shop. Tape one end with brown paper tape to keep the face and end located (**3–3**) and the other tape with perforated tape so that the two will not be confused. Paper tape is discussed on page 55.

Either return long slices to the shipping box or construct a short tube of single-side or cardboard. As for short slices, you can store them in the shipping envelope they arrived in (**3–4**).

Flattening Techniques

One of the frustrations of using raw veneer is that it's not always flat. This is especially true of figured cuts—burls, crotches, stump wood, etc. Some of these cuts are wrinkled to such a degree that an attempt to force them flat in a dry state will cause severe breakage. Even vertical-grain veneer, if not properly stored, can have waves or be cupped to a degree that it will split if forced flat. Cutting, fitting, taping, and bonding wrinkled veneer is all but impossible. Irregularities must be dealt with before any work can be done.

There is a reason for veneer distortion. When veneer is sliced, it is usually in a saturated, warm condition. As the slice dries, different areas—such as various sections of burls and crotches—shrink to various degrees, accounting for the wrinkled condition.

The first stage in any flattening process is to render the veneer as pliable as possible, or plasticize it. This will permit some areas to stretch and others to compress when the veneer is eased into a flat condition.

One effective method of plasticizing wood is to expose it to gaseous ammonia under pressure. The drawbacks to this method are that the equipment required is expensive, the ammonia is dangerous, and the discoloration resulting in some species is impossible to reconcile.

3-4. This shipping envelope provides a storage container for short slices.

Common products such as fabric softener and hair conditioner can be used instead of ammonia to plasticize wood. When mixed with water, these products do an excellent job. Their drawback is the residue left behind. The silicone in fabric softener, for instance, will render the veneer almost impervious to many bonding adhesives, and, if that's not bad enough, any surface coating applied to the veneer will orange-peel and fish-eye to a most unacceptable degree. Hair conditioners are not as bad as fabric softener, but the residues may have long-term effects on any finishing system used.

There is a better alternative: Water. Water alone will plasticize wood to a great degree. Water mixed with glycerin works even better. And adding alcohol makes the mixture even more effective.

Wood that has been heated to 150°F. or higher is far more pliable than wood at room temperature. Heat alone will relax the fibers of wood, allowing it to take on a new shape and keep it.

Time is another factor. Wood can be encouraged to change dimension, but this encouragement must be applied gently and lovingly over a period of time.

Below are techniques for successfully for flattening veneer in the small shop.

Minor Flattening

If the veneer is not seriously wrinkled and the bonding agent used will be hot hide or "dry" glue, little flattening is required. About a minute after the hot hide glue is applied to the veneer, it becomes as limp as a dishrag. This is true even of large mahogany crotches. Invariably, however, there will be a couple of spots about the size of a quarter that will

3-5. Deep-reach clamp holding down a troublesome spot.

refuse to go down. For these little annoyances, keep some deep-reach clamps handy (**3–5**).

Flattening Veneer with a Household Iron

If you are using adhesives other than hot hide glue—and the material is not seriously wrinkled—pressing with a household iron works well. A steam iron is effective, but a spray bottle and a standard iron are more versatile. In addition to figured species, the iron can also quickly flatten vertical-grain slices that are too cupped to work with. It is also useful in restoration work to put down small, loose spots and heavy grain that has been raised in the stripping and washing process.

To flatten with an iron, spray both sides of the veneer with warm water. Then give a second coat to concave areas of figured cuts or the concave side of vertical-grain cuts (**3–6**); this begins the flattening process by expanding the "short" side. With the iron set

3-6. Spraying the concave side of veneer.

3-7. Supporting an iron's weight when flattening veneer.

on medium, slowly apply heat while supporting most of the iron's weight (**3–7**). Turn the veneer frequently and work both sides. As the veneer becomes flatter, more and more of the iron's weight can be applied to it. Continue pressing until the veneer is thoroughly flat and dry.

When using a steam iron, as the veneer becomes flat turn off the steam and continue ironing until the veneer is dry. Remember, never force the iron when flattening veneer.

Flattening Veneer with a Hot Press

Refer to Bonding Using Mechanical Presses on pages 96 to 98 for a complete description of flattening with a hot press.

Flattening Veneer with Water, Glycerin, and Alcohol

Another method—and perhaps the most time-honored—is to spray the veneer with a mixture of water, glycerin, and alcohol. Here, water is the plasticizer. Glycerin serves as a wetting agent and its hygroscopic properties (ability to readily absorb moisture from the atmosphere) will force the wood to hold some moisture, keeping it pliable. The alcohol speeds drying. One large veneer supplier recommends this formula: one gallon water, eight ounces glycerin, eight ounces alcohol.

Some people suggest mixing in such things as flour and glue. These components will add some strength to the veneer and help keep it flat, but it may not be worth the added mess.

Although the water will work by itself, if you live in a warm, damp climate and drying will take many days, add alcohol. It will act as a disinfectant. Without it, you may find all kinds of "stuff" growing in the veneer.

Caution: Should you apply heat to veneers with residues of glycerin or alcohol—either from an iron or from the steam process described below—there will be some unhealthy fumes generated. *Work in a well-ventilated area and, at the first sign of discomfort, open all doors and windows and leave the area until the fumes have cleared.*

3-8. Flattening veneer using a water/alcohol/
glycerin mixture.

In practice, spray both sides of the veneers to be flattened with a heavy coat of the water/alcohol/glycerin mixture (**3–8**). Then place the veneers between two pieces of ³/₄-inch-thick particleboard. The coated particleboard favored by kitchen cabinet manufacturers is especially useful because the coating prevents the water from penetrating to the particleboard and eventually destroying it. Next, place a weight on the stack in increasing amounts as the mixture disperses, penetrates the veneer, and the veneer begins to flatten. Finally, place several clamps around the edges of the particleboard and a deep-reach clamp in the center (**3–9**). All of this takes place over a period of an hour or more. Depending on the tenacity of the veneer, the stack is often clamped overnight.

Clamping as soon as the veneer is reasonably flat is important because it limits the movement of the veneer, causing compression rather than expansion. Many woods will compress up to 20 percent without failure, while expansion of as little as five percent may result in splitting.

Flattening Veneer with Steam

Steam works great for flattening veneer. Two methods for generating steam are mentioned in Chapter 6. Carefully consider these, as steam has many uses in the small shop.

If flattening veneer with steam, spray the pieces with warm water on both sides, stack them, and place moderate weight on the stack for an hour or so. Until the water penetrates fully, the veneers will be somewhat brittle. You don't want to use so much weight that they will fracture. Spraying the pieces with warm water, stacking them, and placing moderate weight on them provides for some initial flattening and allows the water to disperse throughout the veneer.

Next, place the veneers—usually no more than two at a time—in a shallow box

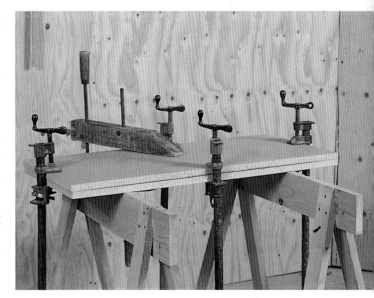

3-9. Clamping procedures when flattening veneer.

3-10. Shop-made steam box for flattening veneer.

constructed of lightweight exterior plywood at the top and bottom, and with ³/₄-inch-thick material screwed to the plywood, forming the sides (**3–10**). Space the veneers from the bottom of the box—or from each other, if you have stacked several slices in a box—with small cubes of ³/₄-inch material, permitting free circulation of the steam. The steam box should rest on a piece of foam insulation. This, in combination with another piece placed over the lid, helps substantially to raise the temperature of the box. Introduce the steam into the box at such an angle that it will flow in a circular fashion.

After three to five minutes in the steam box, the veneer becomes quite limp. The heat also drives some of the moisture from the veneer. It is important to not oversteam the veneer, since this makes it brittle.

As a precaution against burning yourself when using the steam box, wear a light jacket and gloves to remove the heated veneer, while keeping your face well clear of the box.

Although there is little steam pressure involved, a large volume of hot steam is released when the lid is lifted.

Quickly place the veneer slices between pieces of particleboard and clamp them or place a heavy weight on them until they are cool. When they have cooled, proceed with the drying process.

Drying Technique

After flattening, veneers must be dried before they can be used. Many people recommend placing the veneer between layers of newspaper, weighting the stack, and periodically changing the newspaper. If you do not want to periodically change newspaper between veneers, you can use a product called "single-side." (Drying veneer between sheets of newspaper can sometimes lead to problems. It's possible to set veneer to dry between the pages of a freshly printed newspaper for several days, only to find that the residual alcohol in the veneer softening the uncured printer's ink is carrying it deep into the veneer. Removing the ink can be accomplished by a lot of scrubbing with lacquer thinner and a prodigious amount of sanding.)

Single-side cardboard is a corrugated cardboard with paper applied to only one side of the corrugations. It is relatively inexpensive and readily available from those engaged in the packing and shipping industry.

If using single-side cardboard, place each cut of veneer between two pieces with the corrugations against the veneer and all corrugations running in the same direction (**3–11**). In the case of burls and crotches, rather than stack them in order rotate each 180 degrees, providing more evenly distributed pressure as the material dries and tries to resume its wrinkled condition.

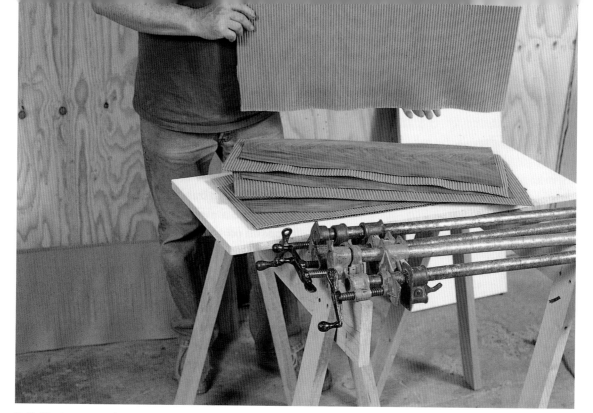

3-11. Placing veneer between corrugated cardboard.

Next, place the stack of veneer between the particleboard pieces and clamp them with moderate pressure, in no way flattening the corrugations of the single-side cardboard. Clamps are important, because there is nothing more frustrating than to see the stack expand as it will if there is only a single, lightweight object on it.

To speed the drying, situate a fan so that it blows air through the corrugations of the single-side cardboard (**3–12**); leave the fan in place for one to three days. (The exact time will depend on the ambient humidity. The times given here are related to the very dry climate of northern Utah.) On the last day, every hour or so, blow hot air from a hair drier through the stack. (Avoid hot air until the last day because this will cause too rapid a drying, which causes excessive checking and splitting.) If you feel that any of the veneer is still moist when disassembling the stack, reassemble the stack and

3-12. The air blown by the fan over a period of three days will speed veneer drying.

continue the hot-air-and-fan treatment for another day or as long as it takes.

It is extremely important that the veneer

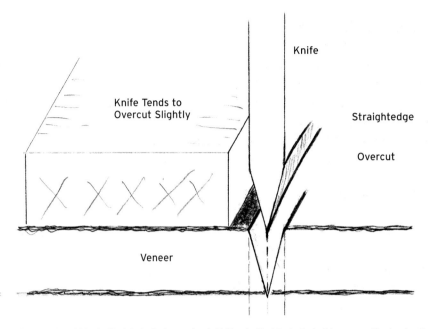

3-17. The cutting angle of the knife blade is important. If the knife blade is held perpendicular to the surface, the veneer will look slightly overcut.

will show that the veneer appears slightly overcut (**3–17**), and, if a guide is being used, the finished cut will be away from the edge of the guide by half the thickness of the blade. Therefore, it is best to tip the knife slightly to the waste side and slightly into the guide.

Always try to place your straightedge or other guide *opposite* the waste. Should the cutting tool wander—which does happen—it wanders into the waste. You will often find yourself cutting joints after a piece has been partially bonded; this is no place for a cutting tool to wander into the workpiece.

It's always best to cut with the grain, but, taking many things into consideration, this is not always possible. Cuts made against the grain are very possible, provided a sharp cutting tool is used. With a sharp tool, you'll need take little notice of the grain direction.

Shooting

Cuts don't always come out perfect. A veneer saw will often leave the edge a little too ragged for a joint. Often a slight sliver will be torn from the workpiece. A miter cut in a border piece might not fit as well as anticipated. The straightedge may have drifted slightly while a cut was being made. In these cases, slight adjustments can be made to a cut with a process called "shooting."

Shooting consists of running a hand plane over the edge of the veneer to true it, just as you would run a plane over the edge of a sawn board. Many craftsmen do this as a matter of course. If you keep your tools sharp, you can eliminate this step and the time it takes—and only resort to it for adjustments and the removal of small defects.

Many woodworking books and magazine articles contain information on building shooting boards that hold the veneer securely and provide a guide surface to hold a hand plane square and true. The problem with many of these shooting boards is that the plane, even though razor sharp, has a tendency to tear the edge of some species of wood, and is even more aggressive on burls, crotch, and stump wood. When using such a shooting board, it is better to substitute a hand plane with a block of wood with 80-grit sandpaper glued to it; this eliminates the tearout. You can also let the veneer hang slightly over the bench—or substrate—and support it with a straightedge for shooting with the sandpaper block. This will eliminate the need for a shooting board altogether.

Shooting a piece of veneer that is hanging over the bench takes a little practice. Remember to keep the overhang to a minimum—not more than $1/8$ inch—hold the block for a square cut, and apply pressure exactly perpendicular to the edge of the veneer (**3–18**). Try this method and you won't have to clutter your shop with yet another jig.

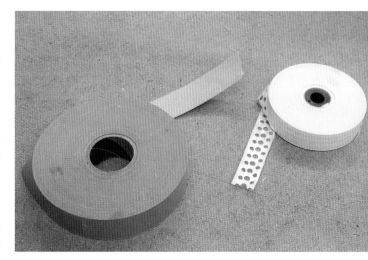

3-19. Types of veneer tape.

TAPING VENEER PIECES

Once the pieces are cut, you may find it necessary to tape several together before bonding. Following is information on this process.

Types of Tape

There are three types of tape that are helpful in veneer work. The first of these is a solid gummed paper tape about 1 inch wide and about .004 inch thick (**3–19**). This is a very good general-purpose tape for holding various pieces of veneer together prior to bonding. This tape should be used on the surface only. If it winds up in the glue line, the strength of bond will be only as good as the bond between the tape and the veneer, which is nowhere as good as the bond between the bonding adhesive and the veneer.

If you are going to bond the veneer using a press, do not place more than three layers of intersecting tape on the surface of the veneer. This buildup—about .012 inch thick—will leave the area beneath the tape starved for glue while leaving the area around the taped area with an unduly thick glue line.

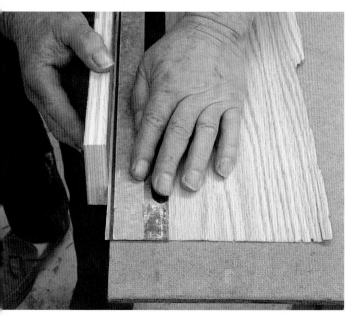

3-18. Preparing the edge for a joint with a shooting block.

3-20. Wetting veneer using a cup and sponge.

3-21. Placing short strips to stabilize a joint.

A second type of gummed paper tape is perforated and much thinner—about .002 inch thick and ¾ inch wide (**3–19**). This type of tape may be left in the glue line, as the bonding adhesive can reach the veneer through the perforations. It's a good tape to use for repairs of splits and tears when you're not sure which side will end up in the glue line. Another advantage of perforated tape is that you can see much of what you are taping through the perforations.

Perforated tape is not as strong as solid tape, but is recommended for jobs when maximum strength is not required. Another disadvantage is that it will permit bleed-through of the bonding adhesive to the surface of the veneer at joints. Consider the whole veneering process before you choose a tape.

You will need some method of wetting both types of tape. One way is to use a cup with a sponge stuffed in it and which is filled almost to the top with water (**3–20**). Passing the tape between the sponge and your fingers gets the tape sufficiently wet. Often you can pump the sponge by pressing on it a couple of times to bring more water to the surface. Get the tape as wet as possible without actually dipping it in water.

The third type of tape that is useful when veneering is plain masking tape. Use it only as a temporary fix in situations where you need a third hand. Masking tape is not really strong enough to firmly hold pieces of veneer together in preparation for bonding. Ironically, however, if it is put into a press, it will hold so well that it will tear fibers from the face of the veneer. Heating the masking tape and pulling it back across itself can minimize this property.

Applying Paper Tape

One of the greatest uses of paper tape is taping seams or joints, so let's deal with that. Once the veneers to be joined have been cut and passed over with a shooting block when necessary, hold them in place with weights, pins, clamps, etc. It's recommended that you put some strips about 2 inches long across the joint at about 6-inch intervals (**3–21**). It is much easier to control the joint in a small area than trying to deal with the whole thing at once. Other than helping you control the joint, the strips have another plus. As the wet paper dries, it shrinks and will pull the joint tightly together.

Press these strips firmly to the veneer with your fingers, a putty knife, or the back of a floor-covering knife. There should be no bubbles or other loose spots in the tape. If there are, read on.

It will take the tape from five to 15 minutes to dry, but you don't have to wait for this. Set your household iron at one-quarter heat. After the tape has set for about 15 seconds, iron it until it has a firm hold of the veneer and is dry—five to ten seconds should do the job (**3–22**). If you have encountered loose spots or bubbles in the tape, wet the surface of the tape and iron. The moisture from the surface will reach the glue and bond the tape.

Once you have the strips in place, make a pencil mark on them about ½ inch from the joint (**3–23**). This will help you locate the strip of tape that you will now run down the length of the joint.

The above described technique also works well for repairing splits caused by rough handling. Just be sure that the split fits

3-22. Drying veneer tape with a household iron.

3-23. Marking veneer for placement of tape.

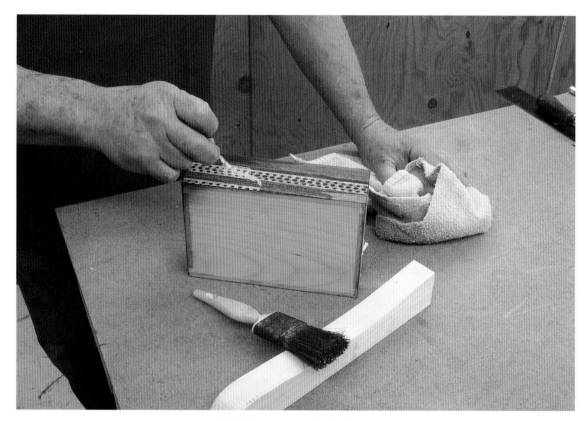

3-24. Removing moistened tape.

together well before beginning. You may set out to repair a split only to find halfway down it that there is a large sliver missing.

Tape Removal

It seems such a shame that after going to all of the work to apply that tape, you must remove it after bonding. You could sand it off. However, sanding several seams can be time consuming and the paper is quite tough; it eats sander belts. If you are going to sand off the tape, be very cautious. The paper is hard and it is very easy to dig into the veneer on either side of a joint, especially if the veneer is of a soft texture.

A better solution is to wet the tape and peel it off. Use a brush and wet only the tape. If your bonding process was successful water shouldn't hurt anything, but why take chances.

Wet the tape a couple times with water and wait ten minutes or more for the water to penetrate the tape. Once the water penetrates the tape, the tape peels right off (**3–24**).

Have a rag handy to wipe any wet glue from the surface.

Let everything dry before sanding. Moisture from the tape is bound to have crept into the veneer, swelling it, and the residual glue on the veneer will be soft, clogging your sandpaper. If you have been careful and wet only the tape, a couple hours should be sufficient; however, overnight is even better.

CHAPTER 4

SUBSTRATES

Veneer has to be applied to some type of material. This material, which shall hereafter be referred to as the "substrate" or "ground," can be solid wood, plywood, or any of the various composition materials that are available these days (**4–1**). If the appropriate adhesive is used, wood veneer can be applied to almost any smooth, clean, stable surface—including steel, glass, even drywall.

The proper selection of a substrate is important, as it will affect the longevity of the veneer work. All substrates are not created equal, but each has application in veneering. Each possible substrate has certain properties that should be considered. The following information describes a condition called pull; the many types of material that can be used as a substrate; and techniques for laying out the substrates and bonding them to the veneer.

4-1. An assortment of substrate material.

PULL

In all cases where a water-based adhesive is used, the substrate will be subjected to a condition called "pull." This condition develops because of the different expansion and contraction characteristics of the veneer versus the substrate. Pull must always be considered when choosing the veneer, substrate, and adhesive.

When a water-based adhesive is spread on any substrate, the moisture causes the side with the adhesive to expand, resulting in cupping of the opposite side. In many tenacious substrates this cupping is almost unnoticeable, because the dry bulk of the material resists the expansion of the side. When the adhesive's moisture gets to the veneer, because it has little volume, the veneer can expand to almost the full extent of its capability. After the veneer/substrate bond is complete and the moisture begins to escape, the substrate will shrink slightly, but the veneer will shrink dramatically, pulling the substrate into a cupped condition. A panel only about 10 inches wide can pull as much as $1/8$ inch (**4–2**).

You wouldn't think that a thin piece of wood could undergo such a powerful reaction, but it does. Because of moisture content, wood can expand and contract dramatically. In quarrying operations, for centuries pieces of dry wood have been driven into cracks or holes drilled into the face of mountainsides. When these pieces of wood are soaked, they expand, and the wood splits away some very impressive pieces of stone from the mountainside.

4-2. Cupping caused by pull.

Dealing with Pull

Don't be afraid of pull. It can be dealt with, and in many cases quite simply, as discussed below.

Pre-Cupping

In days of old, large pieces of solid wood to be veneered were intentionally expanded on the side to be coated with adhesive, by bringing them into contact with wet sawdust, paper, or rags. When the substrate was cupped to the proper degree, the veneer was laid with hot hide glue and a hammer. When the whole assembly dried, it would be flat.

This method is still effective with different types of substrate. Occasionally, however, you may have to use dry heat to encourage the assembly into a flat condition.

Sizing

One method to limit the amount of pull is to "size" the veneer and substrate, that is, to give both a thin coat of glue and allow the glue to dry thoroughly. This partially seals the surfaces and will slow the absorption of moisture from the glue used in bonding, thus limiting, for a time, the dimensional changes. If the dimensional changes can be held in check until the bonding glue grabs, pull is reduced or eliminated.

Veneering Both Sides of the Substrate

Today's standards call for veneering both sides of the substrate. This pulls both sides in the same manner, provided that they are covered with the same species of veneer—which is, in some respects, a little costly. The costs, however, can be minimized by using a veneer of inferior grain pattern on the underside of the substrate. And, often a less costly species of similar texture can be used on the under-

known as flake or chipboard and by other names). This latter material is composed of chips or flakes rotary-cut from softwood logs. These are mixed with knots, sand, rocks, broken machine parts, assorted floor sweepings, and glue. This concoction is pressed into a very stable building board that is wonderful for floor, roof, and wall sheathing.

Although waffle board and fir plywood are relatively cheap and lightweight, they have one glaring disadvantage: Their grain patterns telegraph or transfer to the surface of the veneer. The reason this happens is because the spring and summer wood of the logs are of vastly different textures. Residual moisture in these products, coupled with dimensional changes caused by moisture from the bonding glue, affects summer and spring wood to different degrees. When these woods have dried out, these changes become obvious and can even be felt—which can make for a lot of unnecessary sanding.

side, i.e., birch under bird's-eye maple, rift oak under quartered oak, etc.

TELEGRAPHING

Another thing to be mindful of is "telegraphing." Irregularities in the substrate can appear in the surface of the veneer, sometimes weeks or months after the veneer is bonded. In some instances, this can be a desired thing, but in most cases it is something to watch for.

WOOD SUBSTRATES TO AVOID

There are two types of substrate to be avoided: rotary-cut fir plywood and waffle board (also

SOLID WOOD

Solid wood is an acceptable choice of substrate, but if not thoroughly cured, it can present some of the same telegraphing problems as fir plywood. Knots and other defects will usually telegraph. If all the boards in a particular glued-up substrate are not of equal moisture content, one will shrink more that another, and this difference will telegraph. Any glue joints in solid wood will telegraph if not permitted to dry for several days before sanding or when otherwise preparing the substrate for veneering. And, if the veneer and solid-wood substrate are of vastly different texture, expansion and contraction due to normal seasonal changes can buckle or pull the veneer loose.

The reason that glue joints telegraph in boards or edge banding is simple. The moisture of the glue will cause the pieces to swell at the joint. If the joint is sanded before the moisture has completely escaped, when it does escape, there will be a sunken area along the glue joint.

The disadvantages of a solid-wood substrate can be overcome by a technique called "crossbanding." Here, an inexpensive veneer such as poplar or an inferior quality veneer is bonded to the solid wood or plywood across its grain, on both sides. The face veneer is then bonded to the cross-band with the grain running in the same direction as the substrate (**4–3**). An alternate technique is to bond the crossband to the face veneer and then bond the assembly to the solid wood or plywood (**4–4**). With either technique, the solid wood forms the thick core of a piece of plywood.

Solid wood that has been crossbanded and veneered forms a very stable panel. Telegraphing of defects and glue lines is minimal, and seasonal changes have little effect on it, even if the underside is not sealed. This technique came into extensive use around the

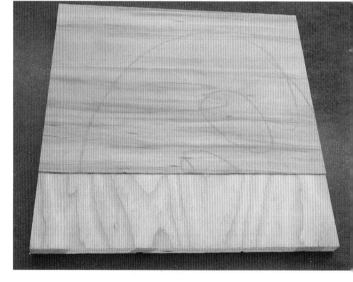

4-3. Fir plywood cross-banded with maple.

turn of the last century and remained popular until some of the man-made substrate materials gained acceptance.

MAN-MADE BOARDS

During the twentieth century, some very fine building boards have been produced that can be used as substrates. Man-made boards are relatively inexpensive, and some have a definite resistance to pull, which is discussed on pages 59 and 61. They are discussed below.

Veneer-Core Plywood

Plywood composed of thick softwood-core veneer with hardwood-face veneer—called "veneer-core" plywood—is a good choice for a substrate. Veneers can be bonded to it either across or with the grain. Hardwood-face plywood is somewhat susceptible to pull, so both sides should be veneered if you're using a water-based adhesive.

Another characteristic to take into consideration is that hardwood-face plywood varies in thickness from sheet to sheet; take care when cutting dadoes to fit a piece of veneer-core plywood. Also, the surface can be somewhat rippled due to telegraphing of the softwood core. While this ripple would go unnoticed on a cabinet side, on an area such as a highly polished tabletop the effect is less than attractive. Veneer-core plywood is used for the blanket chest described in Chapter 11.

Lumber-Core Plywood

Essentially, lumber-core plywood is two pieces of 1/8-thick hardwood-core plywood bonded to the face and back of a solid-wood core of about 1/2-inch thickness. The material is tenacious (it holds stubbornly to its shape) and very stable. Though comparatively expensive, it is not very susceptible to pull, and it's possible to veneer only one side using a water-based adhesive.

Apple/Maple and Baltic Birch

Two more plywood grounds to consider are the very tenacious plywood apple maple and Baltic birch. Both of these are made up of

4-4. Zebra veneer bonded to maple cross-band.

many core veneers of very dense birch and maple. And, both are quite heavy—as heavy as medium-density fiberboard.

Baltic birch is supplied in 5-foot by 5-foot sheets, while apple/maple is supplied in the standard 4-foot by 8-foot sheets. Both have a smooth surface ready for veneer and pulling is minimal only if one side is veneered on the 3/4-inch variety.

The only objection to these products is they are not supplied perfectly flat. Should you design with them, your design should incorporate some sort of frame to pull and hold them flat.

Bender Board

This wonderful product consists of a thin veneer with two much thicker veneers—usually luan—bonded cross-grain to either side. The thick outer veneers often appear to be severely knife-checked or stretched. When bent with the grain, it is very pliable. Three-eighth-inch bender board can be easily bent around a five-gallon bucket—and 1/4-inch bender board around a coffee can.

If you will be doing a lot of curved work, this material will prove invaluable. Take the example of curved panels made with six layers of ⅛-inch-thick plywood. Two pieces of ⅜-inch-thick bender board can be used instead, and although they are not as structurally sound as the six laminations of plywood, they are far more flexible and much less expensive.

Bender board is sold in two configurations: 4-foot by 8-foot, and 8-foot by 4-foot. In the 4-foot by 8-foot configuration, the grain runs as you would expect in a sheet of plywood. In the 8-foot by 4-foot configuration, the grain runs opposite.

Particleboard

This is a product composed of wood particles about the size of coarse sawdust—some refer to it as "sawdust board." It has good stability and is suitable for veneering. When you are using water-based adhesives, minor difficulty may be experienced with telegraphing, as the particles may be of far different densities. This can be resolved by waiting several days until the adhesive is completely cured and thoroughly dry before sanding the finished product.

MDF (Medium-Density Fiberboard)

Probably the finest veneer substrate that has been developed to date is MDF (medium-density fiberboard). This product is composed of wood reduced to its fiber state. The fibers are mixed with a suitable bonding agent and the mixture pressed to form a stable building board that is as smooth and flat as a pool table. In fact, it has replaced slate in many low-cost pool tables.

MDF is a tenacious material. It holds fasteners reasonably well and it glues well not only to itself but also to edge-banding materials.

MDF may, of course, be edge-banded to receive a decorative shape, but some manufactured furniture has its shape cut into the MDF itself. This molded edge is then painted with a gesso and a wood grain is glazed on—definitely unnoticeable to the unaware.

If using this material, be aware that it is very heavy. If working alone, one way to deal with this product is to have the deliverymen stand the sheets lengthwise against the shop wall. When you're ready to cut a sheet, tip it over onto sticks placed on the floor, rough cut the pieces needed with a handheld circular saw, and then trim them to exact size with whatever means is convenient.

Fasteners and Water

Fasteners and waters can be devastating to both particleboard and MDF. Screws driven into the face of these products do hold rather well—especially those with coarse threads. However, hardware screws put into the *edge* of either of these products will not hold under stress. There are "knockdown" fixtures specifically designed for particleboard and MDF, but their effectiveness is unpredictable. It is recommended that when you build with particleboard or MDF you add solid wood to the face of any edges that are to receive screws for hardware and the like.

Contact with water can damage a veneered tabletop in a very short time, even if the veneer was bonded with waterproof glue. If the substrate is solid wood or plywood, often the top can be repaired or re-veneered. If it is particleboard or MDF, repairs are usually impossible. The moisture causes these products to swell dramatically, and even after they are dry, the swelling remains.

Tops are often faced with solid wood after veneering, and sometimes a slight, decorative groove is cut at the joint to disguise it. Water—and it doesn't take much—seeping into that groove will cause both the wood and substrate to swell. When things dry out, the wood shrinks; the substrate doesn't.

Keep in mind the use of the final product and your client's tendency to care for it when determining which substrate material to use.

OTHER SUBSTRATES

Good substrates for wood veneer are not limited to wood or wood products. There are other grounds that can be used.

Metal

There are times when veneer can be bonded over metal, as in the example of a steel filing cabinet veneered with oak. In this case, contact cement and paper-backed veneer are used. One advantage is that it is less expensive than a solid-wood filing cabinet.

Glass

Strips of veneer can, for example, be bonded to window glass to simulate muttons and mullions. In this case, cyanoacrylate glue or contact cement can be used. However, when contact cement is used, the windows may look okay from the face side, but unattractive from the rear.

Drywall

It's possible, for example, to bond pieces of paper-backed oak veneer to drywall. The veneer can then be framed with pieces of solid oak, and a chair rail is place over the frame. This is economical and aesthetically pleasing wainscot.

LAYOUT TECHNIQUE

Layout is the stage where you indicate the location of joints, grain direction, and the presentation of the veneers. It is essentially drawing in full scale. For the most part, it is prudent to do the layout drawing and planning on the substrate. Why waste paper or some other medium when you have a big, clean surface to work with?

While it's always useful to lay out the location of joints, borders, etc., on square and straight-line work, this is not addressed here, as it is so straightforward. Rather, below are useful ways to lay out irregular shapes.

Circles

Circles are very easy to make on the layout using a compass. A compass has one leg with a point and a leg that holds a pencil. Just place the point leg on the center of the circle and swing the pencil throughout the desired radius.

Do not draw a circle with a pin, pencil, and string. The string stretches too much. If you must use this technique, use wire instead of string. Fine wire used for hanging small pictures works very well.

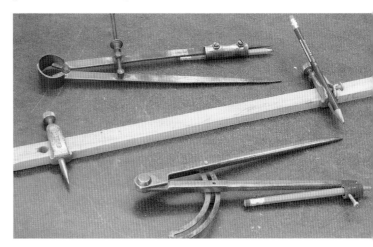

4-5. Compasses and trammel points.

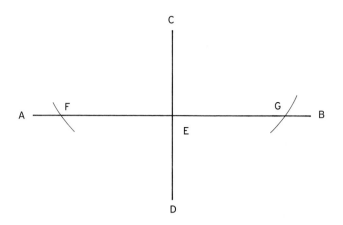

4-6. Method for drawing an oval.

AB to equal the length and CD to equal the width (**4–6**), intersecting perpendicularly at the center of each; call this point E. With a compass or trammels, draw an arc from point C which has a radius equal to AE and which will intersect AB—call these intersections F and G. Drive small nails at F, G, and C. Stretch a loop of fine wire or string around the three points and secure the ends. Then remove the nail from point C, insert a pencil, and draw the oval.

More effective for drawing large-diameter circles—and sections of such circles—is a pair of trammel points (**4–5**). Trammels clamp to a stick of any convenient length and usually consist of one point that can be set in the work and another that will hold a pencil, knife, or scribing device. The fact that a knife can be substituted for the pencil can be very useful for cutting either patterns or the veneer itself. In Circle Devices on pages 40 and 41, I presented some ideas on building your own very economically.

Ovals

An oval is a circle that has been tipped, so a quick way to make a small oval is to draw a circle and tip it. Make the circle with a diameter of the maximum dimension of the oval, out of a substantial material—cardboard, plastic laminate, thin plywood, etc. Lift an edge of the circle until the base of a right triangle formed by the circle as its hypotenuse equals the second or smaller dimension of the oval. Use this as an "eyeball" guide for drawing. There is another way to draw an oval that is easier on larger products. Given the dimensions of the oval, on the substrate draw line

Irregular Curves

There may be a time when you will have to draw curves of specific dimensions. Drawing curves freehand will work. One little trick is to anchor your wrist or elbow—that is, hold it firmly to the drawing surface—and move just at the joint (**4–7**). Often the lines are not smooth and flowing. In such instances, lay out all the fixed dimensions. Then draw the curves desired freehand, as best you can. To check the drawings, drive a number of small nails along the curved lines. Then bend a flexible straightedge along the nails—band steel is

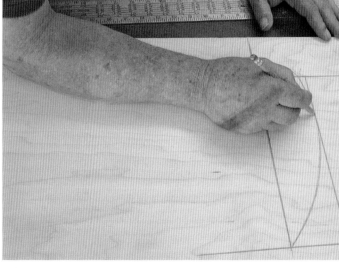

4-7. Drawing a curve freehand.

good for this purpose. Any irregularity will be shown in those places where the straightedge doesn't contact the nails. Use the bent straightedge to draw the final line with a different colored pencil. This technique is used for the kidney-shaped desk and the bombé chest described in Chapters 12 and 14.

EDGE TREATMENTS

Veneered panels which are to become table or cabinet tops and which use particleboard, plywood, or MDF as a substrate will need some sort of edge treatment. No one wants to look at the edge of a piece of particleboard or plywood in the finished product. Even the edges of panels that form frameless cabinet sides need edge treatment. Molded tabletop edges and veneered raised panels will need some form of solid wood to receive the shape.

In some instances, the face veneer may be rolled and formed over an edge in one continuous piece. Even molded edges may be veneered by "upholstering" them with the face veneer. This process is tricky and requires considerable skill and knowledge of the veneer being worked. Rolling face veneer over an edge is used on the lamp and blanket chest projects described in Chapters 10 and 11.

Solid Wood

If your project calls for veneering over solid wood, no special treatment may be required, provided that the substrate and veneer have similar characteristics, e.g., oak veneer over a poor-quality oak substrate. The caution here is to be careful to avoid defects that will appear at the edge. A beautiful, vertical-grain face veneer flowing into a knot on the edge ruins the effect. And, if the edge is to be molded, you don't want to be running a shaper or router through knots and other defects that are likely to cause tear-out.

Many finishing techniques will disguise the character of the wood in an area as small as an edge. If your finishing ability is such that you feel unable to disguise the edge, there is the option of gluing a narrow piece of the chosen species to all edges that are sufficiently wide to accept the decorative molding.

In gluing pieces around a panel that has a solid-wood substrate, consideration of the end grain is important. A narrow board glued lengthwise across end grain is a poor choice. Movement of the substrate across the grain will be far greater than the movement of the narrow board glued to it lengthwise. Within just a few seasonal changes, the substrate will tear the narrow board loose. If this doesn't happen, the narrow board on the end can cause the substrate to check, usually also causing the veneer to check at the same time.

Plywood and Composition Boards

If the panel is to receive a decorative edge, plywood and composition boards should be edge-faced with solid wood. Even if they are not going to receive a shape, facing with solid wood is a good choice. If veneer is glued directly over the edge of plywood, the various bands of end and flat grain can telegraph to the surface of the veneer. Also, a careful examination of the edge of particleboard will reveal that the density of the face sides is greater than the center. This can telegraph, leaving a slight cup in the facing veneer. The edge of MDF may be directly veneered, but if the piece is to receive very rough use, consider edge-banding with solid wood.

When working with plywood and composition boards, all edges may be treated

4-8. Facing a ground by simple edge-gluing.

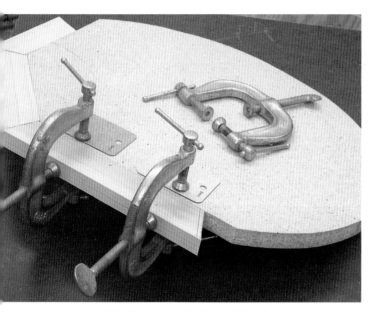

4-9. Facing a ground using edging clamps.

equally. Seasonal, dimensional changes will be the same for the substrate as the face material. The face may be edge-glued directly to the substrate or a joint of some sort may be used. A tongue-and-groove joint works well, and even a spline is adequate.

In facing without a joint, narrow strips of wood are spread with glue and clamped to the face of the substrate. Bar clamps that will span the substrate are always good to use (**4–8**). In instances where a bar clamp is impractical, edging clamps may be used (**4–9**). When using edging clamps, be careful not to mar the surface that will be veneered—the marred areas will need to be patched.

In practice, use glue joints only when there is a lot of facing to do. The joint is used more to locate the facing rather than for strength. One way to make the tongue-and-groove joint is to run the facing sticks through a molder (an automatically fed machine that is capable of cutting all four sizes of a board or stick at once) that sizes them and cuts a tongue. The groove in the substrate can be cut with a router set so that the facing will stand a couple of thousands of an inch above the substrate.

If a molder is not available and you will be using a shaper or router to form the tongue, here are some suggestions: First, face the boards that you will be taking your cuttings from. It is important that they be as straight and flat as possible to start with. This may seem counterproductive in that the pressures in the wood may distort the facing strips as they are ripped from the board; but if the boards are not originally flat and straight there is no chance that ripping will end up flat and straight.

Plane the boards to a thickness that is about .010 inch thicker than the substrate—about the thickness of a matchbook cover. (Note: Plywood thickness can vary dramatically throughout the sheet and from sheet to sheet. Measure in several places.) Next, using a router or shaper, cut the tongue—or other glue-joint shape—in the edge of the full-

4-10. Routing a facing groove.

4-11. Mitered facing corner.

width board. Then rip off the desired width of facing. This method is far safer than attempting to run narrow sticks through a shaper or router table.

For cutting the groove or matching glue-joint shape in the substrate, a router is highly recommended. It is far more accurate and easier to handle than trying to "muscle" large pieces of substrate through a shaper or table-saw dado. Set the depth of the router cut very carefully, using scraps to make test cuts. Also, especially when using plywood, run the router on the side of the substrate that is to be veneered. This will ensure that the facing stands proudly from that side (4–10).

The facing at the corners may be butted or mitered (4–11)—the choice is yours. Should you decide to butt the corners, install the end pieces so that they extend slightly past the substrate edges. Then, with a jointer or hand plane, carefully trim them true with the remaining edges. Be sure to "blind" any joint in the side pieces (4–12) so that the glue joint won't show on the ends or on any shape.

4-12. Blinded butt corner.

In all cases, the facing should be at least $1/2$ inch in width. When facing to receive a shape, the facing should be of sufficient width to accommodate the shape plus about $1/8$ inch. For edges that will be scalloped and shaped, the facing should accommodate the scallop and shape plus about $1/4$ inch.

4-13. Dowel-reinforced corner joint.

Where the facing is sufficiently wide to accept a scallop, special attention should be given to the corners. These should be reinforced with a spline, dowel (**4–13**), or even a biscuit to prevent up-and-down movement at the extreme end of the joint. Even though you have made a good miter or butt joint at the corners, a sharp blow could knock the joint loose. Further, a slight dimensional change in the facing could loosen the corner joint—especially a miter. Take the time to reinforce those corners, making sure that the reinforcement is blind and, therefore, will not interfere with any shape to be used.

Round, Oval, and Other Irregular Edges

Dealing with facing on round, oval, or other irregular panel edges can pose a challenge, but all that is required is a little more time and precision.

Facing for irregular edges may be formed by steam bending. (Steam bending is discussed in Chapter 6.) If you have the equipment and are proficient in the craft, go for it. Steam-bent facing has no joints to contend with and can be a one-step operation. Be sure, however, that you let the bent facing dry thoroughly. Keep in mind that any dimensional changes in the facing will telegraph to the veneer.

If you may be thinking of a kerf-bent facing, forget it. All of the patching and sanding of the voids left by the process would not be worth the effort.

An alternative to bent facing is a sectioned facing (**4–14**). Here a circle, oval, kidney shape, or whatever shape is needed is carefully laid out and its periphery reduced to a number of straight sections. Pieces of solid wood are glued to the edge of each straight section. These boards are of sufficient width so that the periphery of the irregular shape may then be cut.

Facings Thicker Than the Substrate

Often it is desirable to have a facing that is thicker than the substrate. This is particularly true when weight is a consideration. Basically, all of the techniques mentioned above may be used to produce a thicker facing; just make the facing board thicker.

4-14. Sectioned facing.

Applying Facing After the Substrate Has Been Veneered

It should go without saying that a facing can be applied with some "show" wood after the substrate has been veneered. The techniques mentioned above would apply in this case.

There is, however, one added technique that can be used where the facing meets the veneered substrate: You can leave an incised groove (4–15). This will break the continuous plane of the veneer and facing, just in case one is slightly higher than the other. The groove will permit a slight variation that will not be noticed. Even a hand passing over the top will have a hard time feeling variations as great as $1/32$ inch.

The incised groove can collect spills. Even though the piece has received a good finish, water standing in the groove can find its way to the substrate. If the substrate happens to be particleboard or MDF, it will swell, and even when the water dries out, the swelling will remain. Although the groove is very effective in hiding slight inaccuracies, it can ultimately be destructive to your project.

Hinges, Locks, and Other Hardware

If the veneered panel is to become the side of a frameless cabinet or chest, keep in mind any hardware that may be fastened to it. The facing should be wide enough to accommodate mortises for locks, hinges, lid stays, etc., along with the screws that accompany them. Remember that composites—even plywood—are not the best at holding screws and other fasteners, so some sort of facing is a worthwhile investment.

Shaping Composites

It is possible to run a mold on the edge of plywood, particleboard, and especially MDF. In

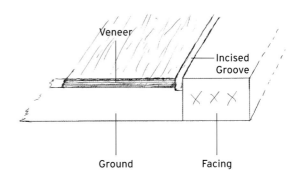

4-15. An incised groove will break the continuous plane of the veneer and facing, just in case one is slightly higher than the other.

the finishing process, this shape is painted with a heavy gesso and sanded smooth. A wood grain is then added to it, using glazes. There are tables with shaped MDF edges painted a brown color—usually a little darker than the color of the wood top.

In shaping particleboard and MDF, you will need to use a carbide cutter. Contamination in the substrate will dull a steel cutter in no time.

As far as longevity goes, be aware that the edge of any tabletop is subject to a great deal of abuse, and the edges of particleboard and MDF are not durable. If you intend to spend a lot of time and expense for veneers, please consider a solid-wood edge treatment.

With regard to shaping composition boards, don't cut so many corners that your work cannot withstand the test of time.

Trimming and Repairing Faced Substrates

Once the facing has been applied, it will hopefully stand slightly above the substrate.

This slight excess will have to be trimmed off, but before even thinking about trimming consider this: The moisture in the glue used to secure the facing has caused both the facing and substrate to swell at the glue line. If any trimming or sanding is done before this moisture has left the assembly, it will cut away this swelled area. When the moisture does leave completely, it will leave behind a valley that will telegraph to the surface of any veneer applied over it as described under Telegraphing on pages 61 to 62.

There may be some defects in the faced substrate. A ding or two that you put in while applying the facing, or perhaps a miter joint that fits less than perfectly, will need to be patched. As a general rule, avoid any water-based patches, as these will need to dry for several days. The moisture from the patch will cause swelling of the surrounding wood, and, if the panel is processed immediately, telegraphing can occur much the same as with the glue line described above.

Also shy away from nitrocellulose putties. They just don't seem to stick as well as they should. Instead, use auto-body putty. This catalyzed filler sets quickly, sticks well, doesn't shrink, and is very hard.

FINAL PROCEDURES

Once all glue and patches are completely dry, trim any facing flat with the surface of the substrate. If the difference between the facing and substrate is small—say the difference of a matchbook cover or less—a sharp scraper is all that is needed. A sharp hand plane may be needed if the difference is greater. If the facing is narrow, a router and a flush-trimming bit will work, or, if you feel proficient, use a belt sander.

In the past, substrates were "toothed," that is, they were passed over with a small hand plane with an iron ground to resemble saw teeth. This was done to provide small reservoirs to hold the hot hide glue that was to be used. You probably do not own a toothing plane, so for substrates on which you intend to use hide glue, drag the teeth of an old saw across the substrate.

Even if you are not using hot hide glue, as a final step completely scratch the surface with 60- or 80-grit sandpaper. This will remove any mill glaze that may exist on wood and break up that very hard and shiny surface on MDF.

The substrate is now ready for the veneer.

CHAPTER 5

BONDING VENEER TO THE SUBSTRATE

For veneering, essentially any adhesive that will stick to wood may be used. By that definition, such things as rubber cement and wallpaper paste are serviceable. However, there are so many adhesives and so many techniques that describing them all could take up volumes, so the information here concentrates on the most applicable and the most readily available, not forgetting economy (**5–1**).

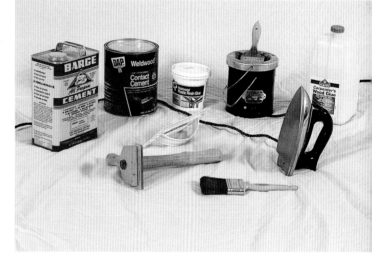

5-1. The tools and equipment needed to bond veneer to the substrate.

ADHESIVE PROPERTIES

Adhesives have different strengths and weaknesses. Consider your project, and then consider the properties of common adhesives, strength of bond, ease of application, water resistance, etc. Never become hard-headed and limit yourself to one course of action.

Strength of Bond

Any adhesive used for veneering should exhibit a strength-of-bond at least as tenacious as the veneer being used. This is a property easily tested. Apply the adhesive to two pieces of wood—according to the manufacturer's recommendations. After the glue is dry, pry the pieces apart. At least some fibers of the wood must remain attached at the glue line. This test will quickly remove rubber cement and wallpaper paste from the list of acceptable adhesives. (Note: rubber cement does have some value in the craft that is discussed in Chapter 8.)

Penetration

Some adhesives such as white and yellow glue penetrate deeply into the wood, while others such as hide glue and urea-formaldehyde simply remain on the surface. It would seem that deep penetration is generally a most desirable characteristic, but not always. While good penetration is most desirable at the glue line, should the adhesive find its way to the surface of the veneer through holes, open grain, spills, or squeeze-out, it can seal the wood, posing challenges in the finishing process.

Shock Resistance

Many adhesives are not extremely shock-resistant, but this characteristic can be beneficial. Glue blocks for many years have been secured with hot hide glue to hold table slides in place. These blocks cannot be pulled loose. Yet, one sharp rap with a hammer will free a block in its entirety, with little or no damage to the table, table slide, or block. A glue's shock resistance should be considered when veneering edges—an area most susceptible to shock.

Hardness

Adhesives used for veneering should not form a pad beneath the veneer, as will white glue and some applications of yellow glue. A panel veneered with a hard species such as maple will loose a great deal of its durability if padded with a soft adhesive. If you have ever torn a cushioned floor covering with refrigerator feet, you are quite familiar with the dangers of a pad beneath an otherwise durable surface. While adhesive hardness can be of little importance on vertical surfaces, it is something to consider on tabletops. It is wise to consider hide glue or urea-formaldehyde for such applications.

Glue-Line Thickness

Most adhesives work best when the adhesive thickness is held to a minimum. In all cases, any veneering process should attempt to hold the glue-line thickness to a minimum. The finishing process will reveal a thick glue line on an edge—especially if the adhesive is of the deep-penetrating type and seals a small area—inhibiting the penetration of stain. The glue line, as described in the section on hardness above, will affect durability of the surface.

Clamping Pressure

It is important that the materials being bonded be held in tight contact during the time that the glue takes to set. The amount of pressure required is often related to the viscosity of the adhesive, as excess glue should be squeezed from the glue line. While generating such pressure may be of minor importance in a plant using a hydraulic press and microwave drying equipment, it is something to consider when working in the cool garage with the mere aid of a few clamps. Most of the readily available woodworking adhesives will work using moderate clamping pressure, but as there is a large surface to be considered in veneering, the more pressure the better. Moisture from the glue will cause the veneer to expand dramatically, and if it is not held in firm contact with the ground it can actually wrinkle.

Gap-Filling Properties

Yes, there are gaps in veneer that need to be filled—especially in veneers where the medullar-ray pattern is displayed on the surface. Gaps are also to be found in veneers where the density of the wood varies greatly, such as in burls and crotches. In such veneers as quarter-sawn oak and lacewood, the ray area may be substantially thinner than the surrounding wood. Here, an adhesive that will fill this gap beneath the veneer is of great value, for it will permit the successful use of veneer that may have to be otherwise rejected.

Shrinkage is closely related to the gap-filling properties, so it should be noted that an adhesive that fills gaps and then shrinks dramatically can pose challenges.

Open Assembly Time

Open assembly time refers to the time permitted between the application of the glue and the application of the clamping process being used. This is an important characteristic if the assembly of the veneers is complicated or if getting the assembled panel into clamps or a press involves several steps.

Open assembly time may be greatly extended working in a cool area or by spreading the adhesive with a toothed trowel rather than with brush or roller. Here, beads that are formed by the trowel will squeeze out fresh adhesive when the assembly is pressed. There is good news and bad news with this process. The good news is that there will be fresh adhesive available. The bad news is that if the beads have set sufficiently to overcome the pressures of the press, they will telegraph to the surface, leaving the pattern of the toothed trowel in the veneered surface. Sanding will, of course, meet the challenge.

Initial Adhesion or "Tack"

Some glues, like urea-formaldehyde, have little or no initial adhesion. These will permit the veneer to slide all over the substrate unless it is held in place with tape or pins. They would be unworkable in any type of process involving hammering the veneer to the substrate. A glue like hot hide glue is initially tacky and becomes even more tacky almost immediately upon being used. This is the ultimate glue for a hammering process. Yellow and white glues have little initial tack, but a few minutes after they are spread, the tack develops to a great degree.

Setting Time/Drying Time

Setting time refers to the time it takes for the glue to "get a hold" on the veneer; that is, the time it takes to render the veneer difficult—but not impossible—to remove from the adhesive. Drying time refers to that time it takes for the adhesive to reach full strength; it does not refer to the time it takes for all the moisture to leave the adhesive and wood.

Setting and drying times are usually set forth in the manufacturer's directions. With regard to veneering, keep in mind that these can vary depending on whether the adhesive sets and dries through the evaporation of a solvent, a chemical reaction, or a combination of the two. If evaporation is involved, and the adhesive is contained in a vacuum bag or under a press, setting and drying times can be considerably longer than if the adhesive is left in the open, as the moisture has nowhere to go but into the veneer and substrate.

The temperature of the work area and materials being used also affects setting and drying times. Heat not only accelerates chemical reactions, but it aids in dispersing a solvent—water included—into the air as well as into surrounding dry wood.

Susceptibility to Heat

A table with a dark finish that is placed in front of a sunny window can become very warm. A hot serving platter set on a dining table can transfer a great deal of heat to the tabletop, even if it is set on an insulating pad. If veneering furniture such as these two examples, ponder the heat susceptibility of any adhesive you use.

An adhesive that can be activated by heat can be very useful. These adhesives are described in Dry-Glue Bonding on pages 91 to 94. You can also use heat to encourage the complete bonding of contact cement when building furniture such as the kidney-shaped desk and round dining table described in Chapters 12 and 13.

Creep

Some glues permit slight movement at the glue line even after they are cured. PVA glues are notorious for this, while urea-formaldehyde and hide glue do not permit creep. This is an important property to consider, because a glue that permits creep can be responsible for joints opening days or weeks after bonding.

Reversibility

The action of some glues can be reversed. In other words, these glues can be encouraged to release whatever they are holding and then hold it again. Liquid hide glue can be reversed by soaking the glue joint with water. Hot hide glue can be reversed by soaking the glue joint with water and applying heat. Contact cement can be reversed by soaking the glue line with the appropriate solvent—usually lacquer thinner. Heat can also release contact cement.

While reversibility can be of great value in repair work, in the overall process of building veneered furniture it can create challenges. One should have the entire process in mind, along with the intended use of the finished product, before choosing an adhesive.

Susceptibility to Solvents (Including Water)

A panel veneered with hide glue—a reversible adhesive—and then drenched with a water-based stain can come apart. Veneer bonded with contact cement can be loosened if colored with a stain and a finishing process using lacquer thinner. Even mineral spirits can weaken a contact-cement bond.

The bond of nonreversible adhesives can often be weakened by solvents. White and yellow glues cannot be reversed, but their bond can be weakened with water.

Usually, a glue's susceptibility to solvents depends on the length of its exposure to the solvent, the strength of the solvent, and any pressure that might exist within the veneer. Flat veneers bonded with contact cement may be finished with lacquer, especially if the initial coats are light and permitted to dry thoroughly between coats. A wrinkled burl that has taken considerable pressure to put down could loosen if given a lacquer finish. And the same applies to water-susceptible glues used in conjunction with water-based finishes.

TYPES OF ADHESIVE

Hot Hide Glue

In the hobby shop, small woodworking shop, and custom studio, hot hide glue is a most valuable adhesive when used properly (5–2). This centuries-old adhesive is made by rendering the hides, hooves, and bones of animals. It is supplied dry, in flake form, and also ground to

5-2. Veneering molding using hot hide glue.

5-3. Reconstituted hide glue.

about the consistency of coarse cornmeal. In adding cold water to the amber-colored, dry product, it soaks up the water and expands dramatically. Each flake or granule turns to a rubber-like glob (**5–3**); the water does not dissolve the glue, it brings it to life. When excess water is poured off, these globs are heated (140°F. to a maximum or 150°F); they melt and turn into a very thick, sticky liquid (**5–4**).

Hot hide glue is nontoxic. It does not penetrate deeply, and relies on surface adhesion rather than deep penetration for bonding. It will stick even to glass.

How Strong is Hide Glue?

A process in the decorative-glass industry consists of spreading hide glue over glass that has been scuffed by light sanding or sandblasting. When the glue dries, it shrinks but holds to the glass with such tenacity that it fractures the surface, creating a design called "glue chip." Needless to say, a product with that tenacity will hold two pieces of wood together.

5-4. Melted hide glue.

Hot hide glue dries quite hard. (It is possible to cut oneself when handling the fractured flakes.) This hardness, coupled with the fact that the glue does not penetrate deeply, makes sanding easy. The glue does not readily clog sandpaper, and little sanding is required to remove every trace of it from the surface of the wood. However, it does fill the pores of open-grain woods to an extent. If your finishing process calls for filler, it's a good idea to remove all of the hide glue from the surface of your project using warm water and a stiff brush.

As it is a dense liquid that dries hard, hot hide glue is a good gap filler. The only problem here is that it does shrink when drying. The percentage of shrinkage can be observed when preparing the glue. Note how much volume the flakes and granules gained in **5–3** as they absorbed the cold water; this should give you an idea of how much the glue will shrink.

Hide glue may be applied to the work using a coarse bristle brush or a toothed glue spreader. Do not use a roller; the glue is just too sticky and will pull the nap from the roller. Whatever spreading system you use, work quickly because the glue must be spread and the veneer set in place before the glue cools. The length of the open assembly time is dependent on the temperature of the substrate and the air in the surrounding shop.

This wonderful adhesive is unique in that it presents two opportunities for sticking to the material. When the glue is first spread and is hot (150°F. maximum), it is moderately tacky. As it cools, the tack increases continually. When it cools to a point that it gels (about 90°F.) is when the glue can first stick to the surface; and the strength of this bond increases as the glue cools more and begins to dry. With effort, the initial bond can be broken, but the glue sticks well enough to hold a flat veneer in place very tightly.

Slightly wrinkled veneers meeting the moisture and heat of the glue become quite pliable, making them much easier to work with. This does not mean that the veneers to be used should not be pre-flattened, but the flattening need not be as extensive. The plia-bility created by heat and moisture makes hot hide glue an excellent choice for curved surfaces, permitting the veneers to be applied with little or no pre-forming.

After overnight drying, the bond is complete, provided that there are no thick areas of glue. These will take longer to dry.

A thoroughly dried (several days) hide-glue bond is not susceptible to solvents used in finishing. Alcohol can soften it slightly, but the exposure must be of long duration—days or weeks. The bond is susceptible to water, but here too exposure must be lengthy.

Hide glue, being a rendered animal product, is susceptible to fungi. Woodworms also seem attracted to hide glue; their holes are far more prevalent in and around joints that have been made with hide glue.

Preparing Hot Hide Glue

Place the dry flakes or ground glue in a container and add about twice the volume of cold water. Stir the mixture to ensure that the water is exposed to all surfaces of the glue particles, and let the mixture stand. After about an hour—two hours for flakes—the hard glue will become soft and will have "grown" substantially. It will not, however, dissolve in the cold water. Pour off the excess water and heat the glue.

Hide glue may be heated in a glue pot especially designed for this purpose. It may also be heated in a double boiler placed on a hot plate or range. The heating plate of a coffeemaker also makes an excellent hide-glue heater. (A temperature of 150° F. is a good temperature for hide glue. Check the temperature of your coffeemaker with a candy thermometer.) Here, place a small pan of water on the coffeemaker's warming element and in the water place a container for the glue. If you don't want to tie up your coffeemaker, try a small Crock-Pot (**5–5**). Here you will have to monitor the temperature as Crock-Pots have only one temperature, on full. Make sure that the glue container is not iron or steel, as any acids in the glue will dissolve the iron and discolor the wood that it is applied to.

No matter how you heat it, never overheat hide glue (150°F. is an absolute maximum); not only will it destroy the glue, the smell is quite unpleasant.

As the jelly-like particles of glue heat, you will notice that they melt and form a thick, sticky liquid. This is a starting point for the glue. Let the glue "cook" until the volume is reduced by about ten percent before using it. If you are working in a very warm shop with warm substrates and can tolerate a more viscous glue, let the glue reduce further. The less water in the glue, the better. Initially a scum will form on the glue (**5–6**). This is often contaminating fat. Skim it off with stick and discard it. Further scum and skins forming on the heated glue can be broken up and stirred back in. If you intend to use a lot of glue, have another container full of glue soaking so that you can gradually add it to the pot.

To test the glue, apply a drop to the pad of your index finger and squeeze it firmly with your thumb. Hold the fingers in place for about a minute, and then pull them apart slowly. This should give you a good feel for the adhesion of the glue.

Cleanup

When working with hide glue, have nearby a bucket of warm water and a wash cloth. Hide glue cannot be wiped off hands and tool handles with a dry cloth or with a cold, wet cloth, but a warm, wet cloth cleans it up easily. A washing machine will remove it from clothing, and a hot shower will remove it from a beard and hair.

An Experiment with Hot Hide Glue

If you are skeptical as to the value of hot hide glue and are reluctant to make an investment of your hard-earned money in an unknown product, pick up a package of unflavored gelatin at the grocery store. This will cost a mere dollar or so.

5-5. This Crock-Pot makes an optional glue pot.

5-6. Scum on a fresh batch of hot hide glue.

Mixing Technique

Always mix urea-formaldehyde in accordance with the manufacturer's directions (**5–7**). After becoming familiar with the product, you may want to vary things a little. It is recommended that you mix the glue in flexible plastic containers. After the leftover glue dries, a little flexing and a sharp rap clean the container.

Cleanup

It is impossible to clean up glue with water after the pot life of the glue is exceeded. (Pot life, also know as working life, is the length of time that the glue retains a viscosity low enough for the glue to be used.) Scraping at this point is recommended, but after the glue cures, scraping often tears out large chunks of wood. Sanding off urea-formaldehyde residue is far more difficult than sanding hide glue, but, like hide glue, urea-formaldehyde residue does not clog the paper.

Keep urea-formaldehyde off your hands, other body parts, and clothing. While it's fresh, it can be washed off with cold water, but after it begins to cure there's no hope of removal. It will peel off skin if soaked in warm water, allowing oils and perspiration to break its bond from beneath. It cannot be removed from clothing once it is cured.

Never dispose of urea-formaldehyde into your sewer system while it's in a liquid state. Not only is it against the law, but the glue can settle in low places in traps and pipes and harden like a rock. Rather, wait until it's hardened and dispose of it in the trash.

Contact Cement

Contact cement is very quick and easy to use. However, it is very susceptible to heat and solvents. It will hold down flat, regular

5-7. Mixing urea-formaldehyde glue.

veneers, but if there are any pressures in the veneers and they have to be forced down, heat from sunlight shining through a window can soften contact cement to a point that it will turn loose. A hot serving platter set on a padded tabletop can cause contact cement to loosen its hold. These conditions can occur months after the contact cement is supposedly cured.

Solvents used in finishing can destroy a contact-cement bond. Lacquer thinner is especially effective. While mineral spirits will not dissolve contact cement, it will soften it. Finishing systems using mineral spirits usually expose the contact-cement bond to the solvent for long periods of time, making matters worse. Due to the glue-line barrier that exists in paper-backed veneers, solvent exposure is minimized, but it should still be considered.

Should a veneered piece ever need to be refinished, the methylene chloride in the stripper is especially effective in breaking a contact-cement bond. If a water wash is used after the stripper, it causes the veneer to swell, pulling the veneer loose in spots.

Another problem with contact cement is that it is basically rubber, and rubber deteriorates over a period of time.

Although there are certain applications where contact cement should not be used, it's a good adhesive when properly used and in situations for which it is suited. Several respected furniture manufacturers use contact cement in curved applications where pressing is cost-prohibitive or impractical.

If contact cement is going to be your choice of adhesives, consider the following:

1. Use flammable-type contact cement. Nonflammable, water-based contact cement can cause the veneer to curl and does not stick as well. Considering the cautions listed on both flammable and non-flammable products, other than the fire hazard, the flammable product is safer to use and has less health risks.

2. Read the fire-hazard precautions on the container of flammable contact cement and follow them explicitly! Remember always that the flammable fumes of contact cement are heavy and will settle to the floor. You may not smell enough fumes to think there is any concentration at all, but your water heater's pilot light will sense the concentration. There is the potential for an explosion.

Make sure that the workshop is well-ventilated and that a fire extinguisher is nearby.

3. Use a heavy-bodied contact cement. The type formulated for the leather industry is best to use.

4. Give the veneer and substrate two coats of contact cement, reducing the contact cement with the manufacturer's recommended thinner or acetone. Lacquer thinner can be used, but the retarder in even cheap lacquer thinners will slow the glue's drying and leave behind residue that will render the adhesive softer than it should be. There are two reasons for thinning. First, the cement will be much easier to spread and second, two coats will ensure complete coverage. To prevent the contact cement from reaching the face of the veneer, let the edges hang over your bench (**5–8**) and brush towards the edges to ensure complete coverage in this important area.

5. Bring the surfaces into complete contact using heavy pressure. A roller is okay, but it should be a small roller that will concentrate the weight of your body on every square inch of the surface. A store-bought or shop-built veneer hammer also works well. In cases where the veneers are wrinkled, a warm iron will smooth them and also aid in the bonding.

6. Let the work bonded with contact cement cure for several days before exposing it to heat or finishing products.

7. Work with very dry veneers. Contact cement permits considerable creep. Any shrinkage in the veneers will cause open joints.

5-8. Applying contact cement to the face of veneer.

5-13. Retrieving a cut-off piece.

5-15. Trimming for a joint.

5-14. Trimming waste from the panel.

5-16. Hammering a third piece of veneer.

ing over your ground. Turn it over, trim away this waste, and get it out of your way (**5–14**). Then turn the ground back over and trim the ends of your two veneers straight (**5–15**). You will be able to remove the waste with a putty knife.

Select another piece of veneer, trim one edge straight, and hammer it into place at the ends of the first two (**5–16**). Here again, after the excess

glue is squeezed out, make a few passes, dragging this piece toward the other two.

Trim the edge of this third piece straight. Then hammer down a fourth piece of veneer that has been cut at an angle (**5–17**). Once it is down, set a fifth piece in place and double-cut the joint (**5–18**). This fifth piece has no fresh glue under it yet. Once the joint is double-cut, scrape away the cut-off piece of the fourth, spread glue, and hammer down the fifth.

Working with hot hide glue allows the craftsman to be creative. You can do anything that works for you.

Continue playing and experimenting until you run out of ground or veneer. But, before you leave the project, spread a thin coat of glue at each joint and hammer down a strip—about two inches wide—of wet, heavy paper (**5–19**). (This heavy paper is very easy to come by and very economical.) The paper on the surface will dry long before the glue in the veneer glue line does. As it dries, it will shrink and pull the joints tightly together.

After the whole project has cooled for about five minutes, wipe the surface down with a warm, wet cloth to remove as much excess glue as you can.

As for further cleanup, your hammer probably has a healthy deposit of glue. Put it in your warm water bucket to soak. You will be able to clean it with a warm cloth in just a few minutes. Remove as much glue as you can from your brush. (One technique is to use your thumb and forefinger.) The glue pot is another matter. There will be some dried glue on the sides as well as melted glue in the bottom (**5–20**). Pour the melted glue out on a piece of plastic film—a trash bag will do. When dry, the glue will not stick to the film and you will have glue flakes with which to start a new batch (**5–21**). Don't worry about the dried glue on the edges of the pot. The next time you use it, soak it in cold water for a hour or so to bring the glue to life and when you heat it, it will melt and flow into the new batch.

Let your practice project dry for three to five days, and then remove the paper. This can be done by sanding—a lot of sanding. It is best

5-17. Hammering a border.

5-18. Double cutting a border joint.

5-19. Applying paper to prevent open joints.

5-20. Note the glue dried on the pot sides.

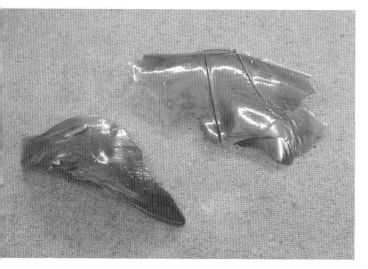

5-22. The finished practice project.

5-21. Dried leftover glue to be reused.

to wet the paper by brushing cold water on it and letting it soak; this could take a half-hour. When the glue on the paper is softened, a putty knife can be used to carefully scrap away the paper. Allow several hours drying time before sanding—overnight would be better.

After the piece is sanded, examine the joints you have made (**5–22**). They should be very tight. Next, observe the pull of the piece. The 10-inch-wide board shown in the photos pulled almost ⅛ inch.

Now you are ready to use hot hide glue on a real project.

Hammering with Other Adhesives

If you have a *small* area to veneer, adhesives other than hide glue can be used in the hammering process. Essentially, any glue with good initial tack may be used, but yellow glue is excellent. The veneer in question should be flat enough that the initial hold of the adhesive is not required to flatten it. Paper-backed veneer is preferable for this type of operation. Here, there will be no glue mixing, no hot-glue pot, and no bucket of water for washing.

To hammer with yellow glue, spread a thin coat of the adhesive on the substrate. Then quickly place the veneer on the substrate and touch it with the hammer, transferring glue to the veneer. Next, remove the veneer by carefully peeling it back and set it to one side. This allows the glue to dry slightly and "tack up." If the squeeze-out is excessive, spread it out with your fingers, trying not to disturb the little mounds of glue on the body of the veneer that were formed when the veneer was peeled back. These will hold fresh glue that will help in the final bonding.

Observe the veneer and the substrate as they set in the open. Depending on the shop humidity, in a minute or so the glue will begin to take on a transparent look. Testing with a fingertip will prove that the glue has become substantially more tacky. At this time, place the veneer back on the substrate and hammer it. If the edges are curling up because of the moisture from the glue, moisten the face of the veneer with clean water. After the curling subsides, hammer it one final time. Set the work aside for a few minutes before trimming it.

This technique takes a little practice, but it's well worth it. Small pieces can be bonded far more quickly than with contact cement, and it goes without saying that the bond will be bet-

5-23. In "dry-glue" bonding, white, yellow, or waterproof PVA glue is spread on both the veneer and substrate. After the glue is dry, the veneer is set in place and heated with a household iron. The heat reactivates the glue and bonds the two surfaces.

ter. I've used this method for years and recommend it highly for small pieces. If the work is over a quarter-foot square, however, heat up the glue pot or choose another technique.

Hammering Irregular Shapes
Hammering lends itself to the veneering of all kinds of irregular shapes. In many cases, the veneer should be pre-formed to the irregular shape before the process (see Pre-Forming Veneer on pages 52 and 53), and often the conventional veneer hammer will have to be substituted with a slightly different device. In all cases, the work can be successfully done without the investment in forms, clamps, jigs, vacuum pumps, or vinyl bags. It requires only you, the substrate, the veneer, a hammering device, some glue and, well, maybe just one clamp to hold the substrate in place.

Dry-Glue Bonding
Another method of installing veneer with a minimum of equipment is by a process called "dry-glue" bonding. Here, white, yellow, or waterproof PVA glue is spread on both the veneer and substrate. After the glue is dry, the veneer is set in place and heated with a household iron (**5–23**). The heat reactivates the glue and bonds the two surfaces.

White glue is the easiest to use. It requires less heat—about 180°F.—and the bond is more complete. Its disadvantage is that it leaves a soft glue line that can act as a cushion under the veneer. This is something to consider in veneering a tabletop that is to have heavy use.

Yellow glue leaves a harder glue line, but it requires more heat—about 250°F. And as it is not as fluid when warm, more pressure from the iron is needed to complete a good bond.

Waterproof PVA takes even more heat—

350°F.—and still more pressure. In that the pieces you build are not meant to soak in water, the finish will protect your work from casual wetness. And if the veneered piece did get wet for any extended period, there would be other damage. It does not pay to use water-proof PVA in any of your dry-glue work.

As the water has left the glue before bonding takes place, pulling is almost nonexistent. This aspect of the process is very appealing.

This method is not useful in all applications. It can be resorted to in instances where the work is of such magnitude that presses, pre-cupping, or veneering both sides of the panel are impractical. The technique permits veneering with one piece at a time, cutting joints as you proceed. It lends itself to making compressed joints that have no tendency to open. Dry glue can be used on curved as well as flat surfaces and is nowhere as messy as hot hide glue. The process does require some skill, practice, and a good feel for the materials, but it is well worth considering.

Preparation

The substrates used for dry glue should be prepared as are those for any other veneering process, but be sure to scuff the surface with 80-grit sandpaper—especially the surface of MDF—to remove any glaze that may have formed. Glaze will often cause the glue to bead up or become "fish-eyed" as it is spread. Also, dried glue tends to separate from glazed surfaces when warmed.

In preparing the veneers, the paper on paper-backed veneers should be scuffed to prevent fish-eye (**5–24**). Wrinkled veneers should be flattened. This will seem redundant as the work progresses, but starting with reasonably flat veneer is important.

Until after the glue is spread and dried,

keep the veneer in as large a piece as you can practically work with. You will find that veneer is far easier to handle and cut with that coat of dried glue on its back reinforcing it.

It is recommended that you thin the glue with water and give the surfaces two coats. Thinned glue is much easier to spread evenly. This ensures good coverage. Thinning also lessens the thickness of the glue line. The amount of water added depends on the glue. White glue requires less water than yellow, and glues from different manufacturers are of different consistencies. In any event, the glue should be the consistency of heavy cream.

It is better to spread the glue with a brush, so that the liquid can be worked thoroughly into the surface.

Spreading the substrate is simple, but the veneer can present challenges. When the wet glue hits the veneer, it will expand one side, making it curl up. To prevent this, keep your spray bottle handy and spray a water mist on the face side of the veneer just prior to spreading the glue. If the veneer still curls, spray more water. Continue to watch the veneer as the glue dries, spraying a mist of water whenever necessary. This is a part of the process you have to stay with—don't spread the veneer and go to lunch.

Some distortion of the veneer is to be expected. If the distortion causes the glue to flow into puddles, spread them out and don't apply the glue so heavy the next time.

To aid in drying, set the veneer on sticks so that it will get airflow on all sides. And to get that air to flow, place a fan across the room, setting it so that it gently blows on the veneer and substrate. Drying time is completely dependent on the temperature and the ambient humidity. In the dry climate of northern Utah, drying takes about a half-

5-24. Passing sandpaper over the ground to remove any high spots caused by dust.

hour. In southern Florida, it could take hours—perhaps days. After the first coat is dry to the point where it has lost its opaque look, apply the second coat. Because the first coat has sealed the veneer, spraying a water mist on the face side is often unnecessary.

When the glue has dried, put the veneer between sheets of coated particleboard to help flatten it and hold it flat until it's bonded.

Material that has been spread with white glue can sit around almost indefinitely before it is ironed down. Material spread with yellow glue should be bonded within a week. If waterproof yellow glue must be used, bonding must take place within 72 hours. In all cases, try to keep the spread materials as dust-free as possible.

In cases where the veneers have become terribly wrinkled—as happens so often with figured cuts—pass a warm iron over the faces to help flatten them. If they're too wrinkled for the iron, heat them with a hair dryer. Then,

while they are still warm, place them between the sheets of particleboard.

Prior to bonding, pass a block with 80-grit sandpaper lightly over the substrate and, if possible, the veneer. This cuts the top off any dust particles that may have settled in the wet glue. Then wipe the surface with a damp cloth to remove any dust. The tiny amount of moisture thus imparted seems to have a positive effect on the bonding.

Bonding Techniques

With the glue dry on both the substrate and veneer, bonding can begin. After setting the first piece in place, tack it in a couple of spots to keep it from moving. If the veneer is wrinkled, pick low spots and, with the tip of the iron, heat areas about the size of a penny. Then, begin to pass the iron lightly over the surface of the veneer. The warmth thus imparted will soften the veneer and the glue, helping to reduce any wrinkles. Increase the pressure until the veneer begins to stick. At this point, the surface should be uncomfortably warm to the touch if you are using white glue and hot if you are using yellow. When the veneer is flat and seems bonded, starting at the center, work with the tip of the iron, passing over every square inch of the veneer.

How much pressure do you use? Don't break the iron's handle. The hot glue is somewhat fluid, and firm pressure will cause the surfaces to mix—which is the desired effect. Working with the tip of the iron will concentrate the pressure and also accommodate any differences in the thickness of the veneers.

If there is trimming to be done after the veneer and substrate are bonded, avoid heavy pressure in the areas that are to be cut away. Bonding that may accidentally occur from light pressure can usually be parted with a chisel or putty knife. (**5–25**). Should the bonding be complete in the areas that are cut away, the chisel work will be more difficult and the substrate will probably need to be spread again with glue.

Joints

Joints may be double cut when using the dry-glue process. Simply avoid bonding about one inch from the joint area. After both cuts are bonded, double-cut the joint, gently lift the top veneer, and remove the waste. Then, firmly bond the joint area.

It is recommended that you do not double cut. Although the glue and veneer are "dry," there exists in the veneer and glue some residual moisture—more moisture than ambient conditions would dictate. When this moisture finally escapes—and it could take weeks—the joint could open, as PVA glue does permit some creep. Experiment. If in your climate double cutting works, do it. In dry climates, double cutting brings only moderate success.

Compressed Joints

A far more reliable method than double cutting is compressing the joints. Bond the first veneer and trim the joint. Trim the joint of the second veneer and make sure it fits the first. Then place a ⅛-inch metal rod about an inch away from the first bonded slice and lay the second slice over it, butting the slices together. Tack the joints down with a couple pieces of masking tape if necessary. Bond the second veneer (except for the area two inches from the joint) with the metal rod under it. Withdraw the rod and iron down the buckle that it caused. Forcing that buckle down establishes significant pressure at the joint—enough to counteract considerable shrinkage.

5-25. Any bonding between the veneer and substrate that may accidentally occur from light pressure can usually be parted with a chisel or putty knife.

The compression technique can even been used to install border components. If there is a small inlay strip in the border, it cannot, of course, be compressed. But the next component can, and this will force the inlay strip tight. With small components, the metal rod is impractical, but these small pieces can be buckled with the hand. Or, sometimes I start ironing from the edge opposite the joint, forcing any wrinkles toward the joint and causing compression.

The blanket chest, round dining table, and bombé chest described in Chapters 11, 13, and 14 present some ideas on dry-gluing techniques.

Contact Cement

There are certain uses for contact cement in the workshop. It's great for on-site plastic laminates, works well for installing cabinet skins, and is the recommended adhesive of the paper-backed veneer manufacturers. Because of its waterproof properties, it is probably the adhesive of choice for veneering a boat.

Where pressing is impractical, contact cement will prove invaluable.

If using contact cement, spread it evenly over the surfaces to be bonded. Blobs of contact cement will telegraph to the surface, and so too will wood or other particles. If you're using a thin paper-backed veneer, you won't be able to sand them out. Two light coats of thinned contact cement are far better than one heavy one. It's not only easier to spread and covers better, thinned contact cement is less likely to form clumps.

It is very important to prevent contact cement from reaching the surface of the veneer. If it does, it can be very difficult to remove. The easiest way to easily spread contact cement is to let the veneer hang just slightly over your bench (**5–26**). And to make sure the edges are well coated, brush toward them.

Let the contact cement dry thoroughly. Do a little experimenting and you'll see the importance of complete drying. Spread contact cement on something and observe it as it dries. As the glue develops a skin, which will make it appear dry, test it with your finger periodically. At one point, you'll find that the skin over the glue sticks to your finger and pulls completely away from the material on which it is spread. The glue may look dry, but isn't. When you place your hand on the contact cement and press firmly, it should not transfer to your hand or separate from the material.

If the contact cement gets too dry—say it was left to dry for a day or two—it will be difficult to get a good bond. The surfaces may be spread with contact cement again or wiped with lacquer thinner or acetone. If the surfaces are dust-free, warming the veneer with an iron once it's in place will help immensely.

Some folks recommend using heavy paper to hold the two surfaces apart until the veneer can be properly positioned. Don't use paper! It can stick and when you pull the paper out, it can tear, leaving sections under the veneer. Strips of plastic laminate about three inches wide and as long as necessary are a far better choice. Placed four to six inches apart, they will hold the two surfaces apart very nicely. Oh yes, they can stick too, but a sharp rap with a hammer on the edge will free them.

Rollers work well for bringing the surfaces together. A veneer hammer works even better. The thin edge of the hammer concentrates far more pressure on a particular area than a roller. One paper-backed veneer manufacturer recommends rubbing the veneer with the edge of a block of wood that has had its sharp edges sanded off. Never pound on veneer with a rubber mallet as you would plastic laminate. It can mar the veneer.

Compressed joints as described in the

5-26. Spreading contact cement.

dry-glue process above work well with contact cement. Use great care when pressing down the buckle because the veneer has more of a tendency to wrinkle and double up. (The kidney-shaped desk described in Chapter 12 presents further ideas on working with contact cement and compressed joints.)

When carrying your masterpiece to the finishing shop, remember that the mineral spirits in stains and varnish can soften the contact cement. Work quickly with the stain. Don't allow it to soak in any more than necessary, and be sure it dries completely before applying any topcoats.

Lacquer works better than varnish over veneer that has been bonded with contact cement. Although the solvent in lacquer is stronger than that of varnish, the exposure to the solvent is far less because it evaporates much more quickly. Spray the lacquer in thin coats and allow complete drying between coats.

Bonding Using Mechanical Presses

Veneering with a press is much the same as edge-gluing boards. You're just working with larger surfaces. You spread an appropriate adhesive and clamp the pieces together.

Chapter 6 discusses mechanical presses in depth. Below are some guidelines for using a press.

Press Criteria

The press surfaces must be flat and smooth. Should you contrive some type of bench press or clamping arrangement and it is twisted, whatever panel put into the press is likely to conform to the twist of the press.

The pressure exerted by the press should be even. Otherwise, it is very likely that pockets of glue will form. These will dry slowly and can cause buckling. They will also shrink,

pulling the veneer down but usually in an uneven manner. It is also very convenient if the pressure of the press can be applied to the center of the work first. This will force excess glue to the outer edges.

How much pressure is required? Essentially, all that is needed is enough to flatten the veneer and hold it in close contact with the substrate. Also, the pressure should be sufficient to overcome any pressures exerted by the veneer as it is moistened by the water in the glue. And that can be a lot.

The press must also be convenient to use. If you have to go through contortions to load the press and apply the pressure, you will subject yourself to great frustration. True, some glues have a long open assembly time, but open assembly time is directly related to drying time. If you would like to press more than one panel a day, make the press convenient to use and apply faster-setting glue.

A press need not be a complicated or expensive thing. For a small project, some particleboard, a few short lengths of 2 x 4, and some clamps will work just fine (5–27). Pass the 2 x 4s over your jointer to be sure they are straight and glue a small square of veneer in the center. This will exert pressure in the center first and will ensure that you do have pressure in the center.

Things to Be Aware Of When Using the Press

When the press is loaded with veneer and pressure is applied, the veneer can slip and slide all over the substrate. Always be sure to secure the veneer in position with paper tape. You can also use masking tape, but it will stick firmly because of the pressure and is likely to damage the veneer as it's removed. To prevent this, gently heat the tape before trying to remove it, and when removing it pull it back across itself.

5-27. A simple veneer press that consists of particle-board, a few short lengths of 2 x 4, and some bar clamps.

In the pressing operation, glue will be forced from the panel. This will definitely occur around the edges, but glue may also be forced through the grain or undetected cracks. You may also have inadvertently transferred a speck or two to the face side of the veneer or the back side of the panel. In all cases, this glue must be kept from sticking to the plates of the press. Keep glue away from the press plates by covering them with a sheet of plastic film; even a sheet of heavy paper helps.

When the veneer comes in contact with the moisture of the glue that is spread on the substrate, it will begin to expand immediately. Very often, the glue will grab around the edges, giving this expansion nowhere to go except the center of the veneer; this causes wrinkling. The wrinkles can become so severe that when the pressure is applied the wrinkles will fold over. The folded wrinkles will be bonded firmly, surrounded by pockets of glue. A spoiled panel is the result.

On the other hand, if the glue has plenty of open assembly time and it doesn't grab quickly, the veneer can expand excessively. As the moisture dries, the veneer shrinks, causing excessive pulling and even checking.

Suffice it to say that the panel must be loaded and pressure applied quickly. If you are veneering both sides of the panel in two separate steps, consistency is also important. Spread the glue in the same density and take the same amount of time getting the panel into the press. The veneer should expand the same amount on both sides so that the pull on the back will be equal to the pull on the face.

The Effects of Heat

All glues set more quickly when warm. Heat, therefore, can be an important factor when using a press. The substrate, the veneer, or the press components may be heated.

Heating the substrate will decrease the open assembly time of the glue, and if that is tolerable in your situation, do it. The temperature of the substrate can be raised considerably by wrapping it in an electric blanket. You can also go over the substrate surface with an iron or hair dryer.

Heating the press components works better in most cases because it doesn't affect the open assembly time of the glue. The substrate may even be cooled to extend the open assembly time. The press plate that contacts the veneer may be heated with an electric blanket, iron, or hair dryer.

Do not leave the electric blanket in the press under pressure. It will be devastating to the little safety thermostats. In addition, the tiny coils of heater wire could be squashed together, causing shorts and setting the blanket on fire.

It is probably better to use a heated metal

plate. Steel works best, because it's cheap and holds heat longer than aluminum. It does need a sheet of plastic film between it and the veneer, to prevent staining. If your press is small, the plate can be put in your kitchen oven and heated—not over 150°F. On a sunny day, the plate can be wrapped in black plastic and set in the sun for a time. When you go to unwrap the plate, wear heavy gloves or oven mittens; you'll be surprised how hot it can get.

One way to heat the press continually with steam is to use a MDF press plate with grooves cut in it for copper tubing. An aluminum plate distributes the heat evenly across the surface. See Chapter 6 for more information.

As discussed earlier, veneer itself could vary in thickness—sometimes dramatically. The flat press plate will hold the veneer against the flat substrate, and the thicker pieces of the veneer will be held tightly to the substrate. Because there is little or no pressure applied to the thinner spots, they will float above the substrate. Hopefully, the voids between the thin spots and the substrate will fill with glue. But what if they don't? In this case, you have an area or spot that isn't bonded, a loose spot, a spot that sounds hollow, or a spot that will be very noticeable under a good finish. A solution is to use a "blanket" between the press plate and the veneer. This blanket consists of a piece of outdoor carpet—that felt-like stuff that's about an eighth-inch thick. The carpet is spongy enough that it takes up the differences in thickness of the veneer, yet is firm enough that it won't permit buckling.

CAULING

Curved work may be veneered with the use of cauls. These are forms which are constructed to match the curvature of the piece being veneered, and which can be thought of as curved press plates. With the hot-hide glue and dry-glue processes at your disposal, it's a waste to expend energy and material to prepare a set of cauls for one-time use. Use cauls only when faced with a large amount of repetitive production work.

Cauls Made from Waste

There are times, however, when the cauls are already part of the work process. Waste cuts can be saved from curved work and used as one side of a caul gluing arrangement. The beauty of saving the waste cuts for veneering purposes is that the width of the kerf removed by the saw blade is the approximate thickness of the veneer, so the piece removed will fit the work perfectly. Further, because the sides of the waste cut and the substrate are parallel, clamping challenges are eliminated. Also, if the curves to be veneered are gentle, preforming can be eliminated.

Waste cuts may have thin spots with little or no strength, but screwing or gluing the waste cut to a flat board or piece of composition material may reinforce these places. In instances where the waste may not be complete, a blanket can be used to take up the slack in the void areas.

One thing to remember when using curved cauls: The ideal clamping pressure is at right angles with the tangent of the curve. Varying more than about 20 degrees from the tangent clamping pressure may not be sufficient in bringing the veneer into good contact with the caul and holding it flat, let alone squeezing out excess glue. Here, relief cuts in the caul combined with some creative clamping may be necessary.

The lamp project described in Chapter 10 contains some ideas on cauling.

Molded Cauls

There are times when a caul is appropriate, but it is too much trouble to make one. In some cases, simple auto-body putty can come in handy. This technique was used to veneer the knobs for the desk described in Chapter 12. Do the following: First construct a small form and fill it with body putty. After placing detail tape over the face of the knob, set it in the fresh putty and allow it to harden (**5–28**).

After a little trimming of the mold, heat the veneer in boiling water, set it over the mold, and then clamp a knob spread with glue over it (**5–29**). It's simple, quick, and economical.

BONDING USING A VACUUM PRESS

Commercial vacuum presses are expensive. For simple, flat work, a shop-made mechanical press will serve well. On occasion, a couple of pieces of MDF and a handful of clamps are sufficient. In situations when very large tabletops are being veneered, you will probably be working a piece at a time. These pieces would not fit into commercially available vacuum bags, and shop-made mechanical presses will not be adequate.

If the veneers you are working with are perfectly flat—as can occur with paper-backed veneers—you will probably have no challenges. But, if your veneers are the least bit wrinkled, the pressure of the vacuum will not pull them down. Any bulges in figured species will just smile at you from beneath the bag's surface. You can assist the vacuum with the use of sandbags or weights, but at times this can be a real hassle.

Vacuum veneering can lend itself to veneering curved surfaces. Here again there are challenges. You must construct some type of form to support the curved surface. This

5-28. A shop-made molded caul.

5-29. The caul was used to veneer drawer knobs.

form must be very stout, for the pressures are tremendous. If you are doing repetitive work, and the cost is spread ou over several items, it would be worthwhile. But, for a single unit, the cost would be prohibitive.

Here are some ideas on how to use vacuum

The concept of vacuum pressing is quite simple. If you put something in a flexible bag and seal it, and then pump the air from the bag, the surfaces of this item will be subjected to atmospheric pressure. This will be about 12-pounds per square inch. When vacuum pressing is used in veneering, this allows the substrate to bond to the veneer. The only equipment required is the flexible bag (usually vinyl), some method of sealing it, and a vacuum pump.

5-30. Making and using shop-made vacuum-veneering equipment. Here plastic film is being folded over to form a vacuum bag.

equipment in your shop. You may want to try out some of these ideas before spending any serious money on commercial equipment.

You can use a real vacuum bag or prepare one from eight-mil plastic film. After cutting a piece of film to the size required, spread a thin three-inch-wide coat of contact cement on the two edges. When trying this in the workshop, you will find that the film starts to curl almost immediately. Don't try to keep it from curling; you'll get glue all over your fingers. Just make sure that the contact cement is spread thinly, and the film will uncurl when it dries.

Next, using whatever you have on hand for slip sticks and weights and something to hold the spread surfaces apart until you get everything in place, fold the film over and bring together the edges spread with contact cement (**5–30**). As a precaution, spread another three-inch-wide band of contact cement down the edges of the bag and, after it's dry, fold the edge over to make a double seal (**5–31**).

Let's assume this veneer bag is being used to bend and veneer a replacement for a chair seat. Spread glue on two pieces of $1/8$-inch plywood and the top of the seat frame (**5–32**).

5-31. Folding over the edge of the plastic film to make a double seal.

That seat frame rests on a piece of $3/4$-inch plywood. If you were to put the frame in the bag without the $3/4$-inch plywood, the pressure of the bag would be exerted on both sides of the

5-32. Spreading the glue.

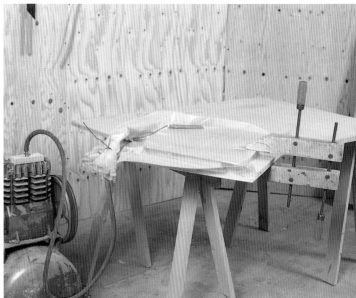

5-33. Using the bag and a modified air compressor to form and veneer a chair seat.

¹/₈-inch material and it would stay flat. If you want the seat to be pulled down in the center, the ³/₄-inch plywood base is a must.

Slide the assembly into the bag, stick the vacuum hose in the middle of the seat, and close the bag by wadding it around the hose and tying it with a piece of bailing wire. Once the vacuum is turned on, it will pull the bag even tighter against the hose, reinforcing the seal. In some instances, it might be necessary to use a hose clamp in order to seal the bag to the hose or wrap the bag and hose with a long piece of rubber cut from an inner tube, but those instances are rare.

Illus. **5–33** shows an air compressor being used as a vacuum pump for the shop-made vacuum press. For an air compressor to compress, it has to suck the air from somewhere, so fasten a block of wood over the intake of the compressor and screw a hose fitting into it. Then open the drain cock on the air tank. The result is a vacuum pump. *If you are using*

an air compressor instead of a vacuum pump, carefully watch the compressor, to make sure that it doesn't overheat.

Tests were performed on this shop-made vacuum press to compare it to "real" equipment. First a stiff spring was placed in the bag with a square block of wood placed on top of the spring. Then the amount of compression to the spring was measured with a ruler. The spring was removed, placed on a bathroom scale, compressed to the dimension measured above, and the reading on the scale was noted. Calculations revealed a pressure of 12 pounds per square inch. This is the best that can be expected from "real" equipment.

Illus. **5–34** shows the completed chair seat.

BONDING CHALLENGES

The biggest challenge you will face in any veneering operation is bubbles or loose spots.

5-34. The completed chair seat.

These can be caused by insufficient pressure on a press or when bonding with contact cement; insufficient heat and pressure when bonding with dry glue; or insufficient spread of glue. The exact reason for the loose spots can be irrelevant when they are found. More important is how to fix them. This is discussed below.

Detecting Loose Spots

After the glue is dry, loose spots can often be detected by passing the edge of a thumbnail over the entire surface and listening for a hollow sound. The points of dividers work even better. Once a loose spot is detected, tapping with a fingernail will confirm your findings.

Another method is to wet the completed panel and carefully examine it under different conditions of lighting. The wetting will cause the veneer to expand, and any loose spots will form some rather dramatic bubbles or wrinkles. Holding the panel up to a light source will show the defects more dramatically and, if the panel is large, a flashlight can be used.

Fixing Loose Spots

If the only loose spots are around the edges, you are truly blessed. Carefully lift the edge with a putty knife, spread more of the bonding glue under the veneer, and clamp the veneer back down. This will even work with contact cement.

If you have used dry glue, hide glue, or contact cement and you find a bubble in the center of the panel, heat is the answer. Heat will not only reactivate the glue to an extent, it will also relax the veneer should there have been pressure that caused the loose spot. In the case of hide glue or dry glue, you may have to wet the spot and let the dampness soak through to the glue. You may also dampen veneers bonded with contact cement. The added moisture will cause the fibers of the veneers to compress, aiding the repair.

If none of the above works or the veneer was bonded with urea-formaldehyde, some fresh glue will have to be added under the spot. Cyanoacrylate can be injected with a hypodermic needle and syringe; a piece of plastic film should be placed over the spot, along with a block of wood that should remain clamped for a time—at least an hour. Other glues will have to be thinned to make it through the needle.

If the bubble is adjacent to a joint, the veneer may be gently lifted with the tip of a knife and glue forced under it. The bubble may also be slit along the grain and glue forced through the slit. Both of these techniques are messy, but often there is no alternative.

No matter what method is used, consider the fact that any glue that reaches the surface of the veneer will seal it and will have to be sanded off before finishing.

DEALING WITH BUBBLES

It's possible that a project will make its way through the sanding and finishing operations before a bubble is noticed. In such a situation, let the finish cure. Sometime when the finish shrinks, it pulls the bubbles down.

If the bubbles still remain, and the glue used was contact cement, warm the area with a hair dryer, being careful not to overheat and spoil the finish. Then place your thumb over the spot, applying all of the pressure you can.

In the case of dry glue, there's no way to heat it hot enough to reactivate the glue without spoiling the finish. In these instances, poke a couple of holes into the bubble with a pushpin. Then put a drop or two of water over the holes and push them into the holes with your thumb. Usually, a bubble will begin to stick as you force the water drops through. Just to be sure the bubble stays down, clamp a block over it with a pad beneath it.

Open Joints

If you carefully follow the procedures for jointing—compression, taping, etc.—you will rarely face the problem of open joints. An open joint was discovered when building the blan-ket chest described in Chapter 11. This was corrected with a tiny sliver.

In cases where you intend to use a similar-colored grain filler, let the filler take care of the joints. If you intend to use a contrasting grain filler, patch open joints with nitrocellulose putty before finishing, letting the putty pick up the color of the stain. Usually open joints occur in border areas where two contrasting woods or grain patterns meet. Here the putty is unnoticeable except on very careful examination.

If you are a purist and opposed to the use of any type of filler or putty, I'll advance one little tip. Provided the opening is small, force yellow glue into the joint from a glue bottle with a tiny tip. After carefully scraping all wet glue from the surface, wet the veneer on both sides of the joint with a brush and water. Be careful to avoid the joint on both sides by about $1/8$ inch because you don't want to dilute the glue. As the veneer expands, the joint components tighten; this will be evident by the glue squeezed out. Keep the veneer wet for about an hour.

The next day, examine the joint components. You will discover that they now fit together tightly. The glue has held. All that remains is to scrape off the squeeze-out.

SHOP-MADE VENEERING EQUIPMENT AND MISCELLANEOUS TECHNIQUES

MECHANICAL VENEERING PRESS

Space will always be at a premium in the average workshop, and ways to make it more cost-effective are always considered. Therefore, any useful tool or fixture that can do double duty is welcomed. That is the case with the mechanical press described in this section. The clamps that apply the pressure have myriad other uses, and the press bench can also double as a stout workbench—if you take special care not to mar the top.

Dimensions

Below are dimensions for a rather versatile veneer press shown completed in **6-6**, on page 107. Consider the projects you have in mind and make adjustments as you see fit. By all means, don't clutter your shop with something bigger than you need.

Top

The table, or bottom fixed-plate, of this press can be made 24 1/2 inches wide x 72 inches long—the 24 1/2-inch width being produced by ripping a sheet of 49-inch MDF in the center. This allows you to veneer tall cabinet sides and doors as well as buffet and credenza tops. In addition, it would permit you to veneer one-half of a 48-inch dining table—a popular size.

Economy also is a consideration. Buying two sheets of MDF, you will be able to get four pieces that are 2 x 6 feet. Three of the pieces are for the table and one for a full-length cover sheet. You will also get two pieces that are 2 x 4 feet; one will be used as a shorter cover and the other as a heater. These are described later.

Base

Build the base out of the most inexpensive material you can find. The legs and spanners shown on the veneering press in this section were made from 8-foot-long 2 x 4s. Eight-foot-long 1 x 6 common pine was used for the rails and stretchers, although plywood rippings can be used. The legs are 30 inches long; they will take up one-third of the 8-foot 2 x 4. The rails

6-1. Truing the edges for the top of the mechanical press.

and stretchers are cut to such a length that the top will hang over the base by 2 inches on all sides to allow plenty of room for clamping.

The stretcher sticks—cut from a 1 x 6 material ripped down the center—are positioned about 16 inches from the floor. You can use the stretcher assembly for storing spanner sticks and clamps.

Stock Preparation

Base

Other than cutting them to length, the only preparation for the base components is to straighten the upper edge of the skirt pieces. Because you want this press to be as perfectly flat as possible, this is an important step. Check the 1 x 6 for straightness against the factory edge of a piece of MDF. If it is not perfectly straight, use a jointer or a hand plane to straighten it.

Top

If you are working alone, you will find the top too heavy to cut on a table saw. Therefore, rough-cut the sheets of MDF with a handheld circular saw and true the edges of the first sheet with a router, using a straight ½-inch carbide cutter with the shank piloting the factory edge of a second sheet (**6-1**). (If you have a flush-trim bit that will cut the full inch, by all means use it.) After the first sheet is trued, place it on each of the others to true them; this will result in three sheets of exactly the same size.

After scuffing the surfaces that will receive glue with 80-grit sandpaper, pull the teeth of an old handsaw over the surfaces, providing "toothing" (**6-2**). This is rather important, as the smooth surface of the MDF will cause the glue to bead up and puddle.

Spanner Sticks

Once the base is assembled and the pieces for the top are sanded, toothed, etc., prepare the spanner sticks. For economy, 2 x 4's will work very well. Once you cut these to length, pass them over your jointer to make sure they are straight. You can use these the same day to laminate the top, but in future pressing

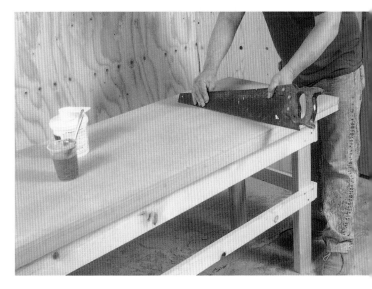

6-2. Using a handsaw to "tooth" the top of the mechanical press.

6-3. Scrap veneer was applied to the center of each spanner for pressure.

operations check to make sure that they have remained straight. It could take a month or more for them to dry out and stabilize. Once you're sure they are dry, pass them over the jointer once more and glue three pieces of veneer in the center (**6–3**). In pressing operations, this will concentrate pressure in the center of the press plate, squeezing excess glue to the outer edges.

Assembly

Base

Fasten all of the base's joints with 1 5/8-inch drywall screws through a small pilot hole bored in the pine. Use a generous amount of yellow glue at each joint. The only caution is to see that the tops of the skirt components are perfectly flush and that the tops of the legs don't stand proud of (higher than) the skirt.

Top

Since you want the press top perfectly flat, the first step is to make sure that the base you are going to glue it onto is completely level. Using a spirit level, make sure that each end is true, sliding a wedge under any leg that needs a little extra length to reach an irregular concrete floor (**6–4**).

Because urea-formaldehyde has no-creep properties, use it for laminating the three pieces that compose the tabletop. In operation, the spanner sticks will be slightly high in the center, tending to cup the top. If yellow or white glue were used for lamination, there is a good possibility that this cup would remain, as the PVA glues do permit some movement in the glue line.

Mix the glue according to the manufacturer's directions. Then add another five percent of water to make the excess glue a little easier to squeeze out. Spreading the glue with a 1/16-inch trowel tipped at about a 45-degree angle will turn it into a 1/32-inch trowel, the size recommended for urea-formaldehyde. After the whole surface is covered, make several more passes with the trowel to ensure an even coating.

After all three pieces are in their correct

6-4. Using a spirit level to ensure that the ends of the press top are level.

6-5. Clamping a press base.

positions, lay out the straightened spanner sticks. Set the clamps in place with just enough pressure to prevent them from falling off. Starting with the center set, begin to tighten the clamps, making sure the clamp pressure is firm and even. The object is to bring the surfaces into close contact, not to distort anything due to excess pressure (**6–5**).

The MDF itself will provide some pressure in the right places. The moisture from the glue will cause the outer pieces to cup. Because the center piece has glue on both sides, it will remain flat. The cupping of the outer pieces will exert increasing pressure in the center of the sheets, and the clamps provide pressure along the edges as the spanner sticks hold the top and bottom sheet flat.

Leave the clamps in place overnight, so that the assembly will have at least 12 hours drying.

Finishing Up
To make it easier to lift that heavy cover sheet on and off the press, you can add a "hinge."

This can simply be a rabbeted stick clamped to the end to the table to prevent the cover from sliding off (**6–6**). Also drill a 1-inch hole partially through one end of the cover sheet to receive a dowel that can hold the cover up for easy loading. A little further on we'll describe a rope and pulley arrangement that will work as well and be a bit safer.

PRESS HEATER
Any shop aid that can speed a project along is a worthwhile investment. Below are two veneer presses with heating plates that can speed up the glue-drying process on a veneered panel.

Solar Heater
This solar-powered heater consists of no more than a piece of 2 x 4-foot x $^3/_{16}$-inch steel plate. The plate is placed on a couple of saw-horses in full sunlight. Within a short time—depending on the season—the plate gets hot enough so that it can only be handled with gloved hands. Once the plate is set in position

6-6. The completed mechanical press. Note the "hinge" clamped to the end of the table.

on the press, it takes over an hour to cool down—ample time for urea-formaldehyde to set with the heat.

Because the plate is brought into close contact with the veneer, and because the plate is steel, it does require a barrier sheet of plastic film between it and the veneer. This prevents squeeze-out from sticking to the plate, and we all know that water + wood + iron = blue stain. In addition, cover the plate with a sheet of particleboard, providing insulation that slows the cooling of the plate.

The plate on my solar heater is slightly cupped—about $\frac{1}{8}$ inch. This is an advantage because the convex side can be put against the veneer and pulled flat with the spanner sticks. This applies pressure to the center of the panel first, forcing excess glue to the edges as clamp pressure is applied to the spanner sticks.

If you are pressing small panels, set out a few blocks the same thickness as the substrate being pressed to support the plate.

Steam-"Fired" Heater
Sometimes there is not enough sunlight to heat your veneer press. The press heater discussed in this chapter provides enough heat. It consists of two separate lengths of $\frac{3}{8}$-inch copper tubing inset into a piece of 1-inch MDF (the tubing layout can be best seen in **6–12**). The two separate "coils" distribute the heat more evenly. Steam passing through the copper tubing is conducted to a plate of .090-inch aluminum that contacts the veneer, distributing the heat evenly. Of course, the heater does need a source of steam. See Steam Generator on pages 114 to 117 for more information.

Cutting the Groove for the Copper Tubing
To cut the groove for the tubing, use a router with a $\frac{3}{8}$-inch straight bit; the shank of the bit

6-7. Cutting the groove for the tubing using a router.

6-8. Inserting the tubing and loop.

should be guided by a template of 1-inch-thick MDF (**6–7**). (A template bushing can also be used for such an operation.) Make the cuts in two $\frac{3}{16}$-inch steps, and on the last cut pass the router several times around the template—hopefully widening the cut slightly.

While you have that router out, you will

6-9. A tubing bender.

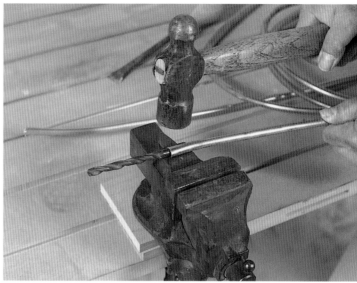

6-11. Tapping on the end of the tubing to expand it so that it can be slipped over the end of the untreated tube.

6-10. Pulling the tubing around the bender.

need to install a slotting cutter and cut some grooves to receive tabletop fasteners. See **6–13** for details.

Placing the Copper Tubing

Inserting the tubing in the straight cuts is easy; placing the loops is not. Here ease the

tubing around the groove, pushing it in with your thumb. Where thumb pressure isn't quite sufficient, use a block of wood and a hammer (**6–8**).

If you kink the tubing, build a tubing bender. This is simply a piece of pine glued to a scrap of MDF. Plane the pine piece to the same thickness as the tubing and cut it to the inside radius of the bend (**6–9**). Next, glue the pine piece and MDF to a scrap of plywood. After the glue is thoroughly dried and any squeeze-out cleaned away, it is a simple matter to firmly pull the tubing around the piece of pine sandwiched between the scraps (**6–10**).

This project uses a 25-foot coil of copper tubing. If your neighborhood home improvement center has only 20-foot coils and no 3/8-inch couplings, do the following: Slide the shank of a 5/16-inch drill bit into the end of a second coil of tubing and take it to the flat portion of your vise. Tap firmly on the end of the tubing as you rotate it (**6–11**). This will cause it to expand enough to slip it over about

6-12. Aluminum foil has been added to the grooves.

¹⁄₂ inch of the end of the untreated tube. It is then a matter of soldering the joint. Needless to say, the groove in the MDF had to be widened and deepened with a chisel at the point of the joint.

Finishing Up

Next, remove the tubing and give the surface of the MDF a thin coat of contact cement. After the contact cement dried, I placed strips of aluminum foil over the grooves—except those for the loops—and pressed the tubing back in, forcing the foil into the groove (**6–12**). This is a necessary step. Without the foil, the heat radiating from the small surface of the pipe is not very effective in heating the plate that is to be placed over it. The foil conducts heat from the bottom and sides of the tubing, and when the spanner sticks press the plate and foil together, the whole assembly works rather efficiently.

Don't expect the foil to stick to the contact cement just yet. It will stick the first time the press is heated, at which point there will

be no chance of it moving about. Until then, handle the assembly carefully to prevent the foil from wrinkling and forming wads. On the ends, beyond the loops, you may want to put a piece of foil into some fresh contact cement. This has no heat-transfer properties; it serves only as a spacer.

Fastening the Aluminum Plate

The first steam-fired heater I built had the aluminum plate fastened with flathead screws going through the plate-and it didn't work! The expansion coefficients of the plate and the MDF were so vastly different that either the plate buckled or the screws were torn from the MDF. It was thus that I resorted to the Z-shaped tabletop fasteners.

Make a cut in the MDF to receive the end of a Z-shaped tabletop fastener. Bore and tap holes in the aluminum plate to accept #8, 32 threads-per-inch screws (**6–13**); if you have spare cabinet hardware screws about an inch long, use them. Use extreme care in boring and tapping the plate. Aluminum isn't the strongest of metals. And don't overtighten the screws.

6-13. Holes have been bored and tapped into the aluminum plate.

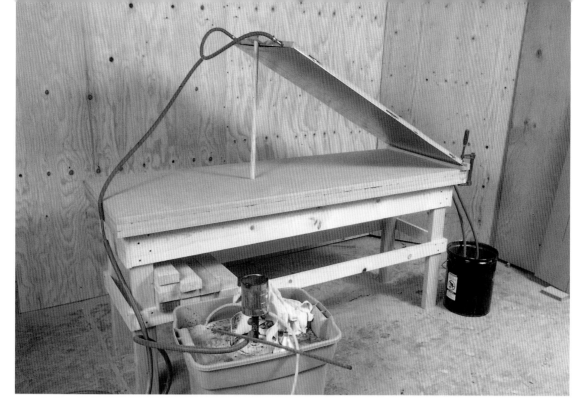

6-14. Using a steam-fired press heater. Notice the bucket on the right, which collects condensation.

On the face side of the plate, cut off the screws and file them flush with the surface. This will allow pressing right to the edge of the plate with no fear of damage to the veneer from protruding screws.

Operation

Steam is introduced into the tubes at the outer edge through a 3/8-inch rubber hose. The outer edge is where the most heat would be needed. At the other end, condensation is collected in a bucket (**6–14**).

Generally, put about a gallon of water in that bucket to keep escaping steam from dramatically raising the humidity of the shop—especially in the summer. Also, steam bubbling through the water will heat it; when it comes time to refill the boiler, you should have a bucket of preheated water at hand.

Leave the press closed until the aluminum plate becomes very hot. This also warms up the table. Although you can put the steel plate that you use as a solar heater on the table and heat it for pressing both sides of a panel at once, the heat from the MDF table is sufficient to cure even urea-formaldehyde.

When the panel to be veneered is set in place and the clamps are installed, the bubbling in the collection bucket will stop for a time. That's because the heat is being transferred to the panel and the steam is condensing.

The steam-fired heater will cure urea-formaldehyde to a rock-hard state in about 15 minutes. Although white and yellow glues don't cure through chemical action alone, it takes about 15 minutes for the heat to drive enough moisture from the glue into the substrate so that the veneer is bonded firmly. Either liquid or hot hide glue takes about an hour.

As mentioned in the section Mechanical Veneering Press, be careful: The stick that holds the cover open can fall on your fingers. Once you locate a place for the press in your workshop, try a different method of holding

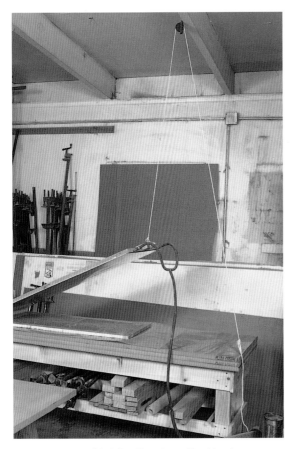

6-15. A means of holding the steam-fired heater open.

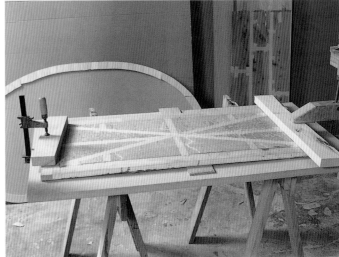

6-16. Using the heated press to flatten a panel.

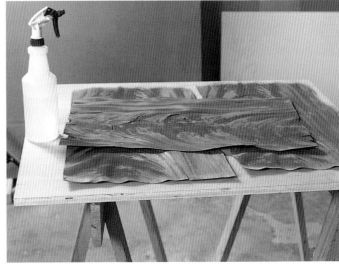

6-17. Flattening and drying crotch slices using the heater press.

it open: String a piece of rope through a pulley nailed to a rafter and tie it off to a screw on the press (**6–15**).

Other Applications

The heated press has other applications: It can be used to flatten things. One of the panels that was pressed for the blanket chest described in Chapter 11 bowed slightly—about 3/16 inch. Because the objective was to make sure the lid of that chest fit comfortably, even this slight bow was intolerable. To correct the condition, the panel was placed in the press for about an hour, and the heater clamped down lightly. Then the heated panel was removed from the press and clamped to a piece of MDF

with a stick in the center, forcing it to bow in the opposite direction (**6–16**). After being left to cool for a couple of hours, it was flat.

The heater press is also an excellent way to quickly flatten and dry veneer. Notice the three wrinkled mahogany crotch slices in **6–17**. Two of these were sprayed with water and

6-18. Plastic film has been placed under the slices sprayed with water.

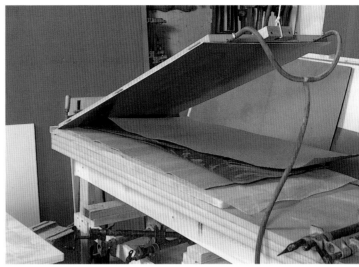

6-20. Corrugated cardboard has been placed above and below the veneers.

6-19. Light clamping pressure is applied to the press.

6-21. The two pieces of veneer are much flatter and dryer than the piece not flattened.

placed in the press. A cover sheet of plastic film was placed under them to prevent the moisture from spoiling the piece of particleboard they rested on (**6–18**). Initially the press was clamped lightly (**6–19**); the clamps were tightened at intervals over a 15-minute period.

Next, the press was opened and a piece of single-side was placed above and below the veneers (**6–20**). Then the press was closed once more. The clamps were replaced with light pressure so as not to flatten the single-side.

Two hours later, the two pieces of veneer were removed. Compared to the third veneer (**6–21**), they were very flat and dry.

STEAM GENERATOR

Before you design and build your own steam generator, you may wish to consider purchasing one. There are two types of generator readily available. One is a device used to steam wallpaper, making it easier to remove. These don't tend to be popular in the United States, but several European Web sites offer them for sale. The other is used for steaming clothing. The larger type—not the hand-held one—will hold several quarts of water. Both generate sufficient steam to operate a steam box for flattening and the press heater mentioned above.

Should you wish to build your own generator, the one described below will last for years. The steam generator is centered around a #20 (five-gallon) propane tank. The finished product is shown in **6–22**, and the components in **6–23**. (There are articles that describe steam generators utilizing paint buckets and even fuel containers. If you opt to use these items, do not

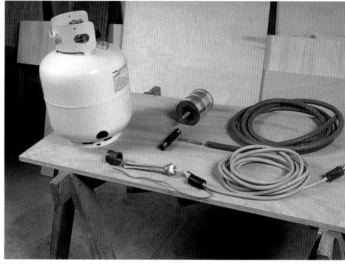

6-23. Components of a steam generator.

6-24. Sawing a hole near the bottom of the tank to receive a pipe coupling.

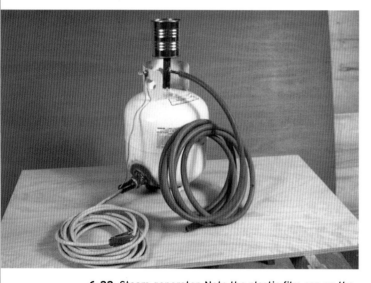

6-22. Steam generator. Note the plastic film can on the end of the electrical cord. This adds a safety dimension. Also, be sure not to omit the green ground wire secured to the handle of the tank with a bolt. If it is omitted and the heating elements "die," thereby shorting to ground or neutral, you could receive a shock.

use lightweight containers because steam will rust them through quickly.)

Saw a hole near the bottom of the tank, and then braze a 1-inch pipe coupling to receive a 1,200-watt, 110-volt water-heater element (**6–24**). In the threaded hole on top of the tank—where the valve was—screw a 4$\frac{1}{2}$-

inch nipple, which serves as a filler pipe. Into the nipple braze a piece of 3/8-inch o.d. copper pipe that will be used as the steam outlet. The tin can on top of the nipple serves as safety pressure relief and as a conveniently removable filler pipe cap. The 4 x ¼-inch bolt—along with the stack of washers—keeps the can centered and prevents it from falling off the filler pipe. A couple pieces of rubber—cut from an old inner tube—seal the top of the nipple.

Filling the can about three-quarters with lead wheel weights gives it enough mass to form a tight seal (6–25). If the pressure in the tank exceeds a safe level, it will gently lift the can and the excess will be released.

Do not set the tank on a camp stove, propane burner, or electric range to use as a electric element. Open flames in the workshop are dangerous.

Construction Details and Instructions

If you have no experience welding tanks, do not do it yourself. Gases can accumulate in the empty container during the brazing process—even if it's a new tank—and they can cause an explosion. This is even more likely with a used tank. Have a professional do the welding. Also, if using a used tank, be prepared for a terrible stench the first few times the boiler is used. If the water is changed every time the boiler is used, the stench leaves more quickly.

Rather than brazing the stub of the 3/8-inch copper pipe into the filler, appropriate pipe fittings may be used, but as long as you have a welder working for you let him do the work.

As you can see in **6–22**, the 1-inch pipe coupling enters the tank at an angle, but parallel to the bottom. Pipe couplings do vary in size, but a 1 3/8-inch hole saw works well. You may have to make a few passes through the

6-25. The components for the electric-fired boiler's tin cup, which serves for pressure relief.

hole with a rat-tail file, and it takes a good blow with a hammer to set the coupling within brazing distance. Measure carefully and chose a hole saw smaller rather than larger than the hole required—brass will not fill large gaps.

You may have some trouble threading the heating element into the coupling, because it has tapered threads and the element doesn't. Wrap a couple of layers of Teflon tape on the element's threads and screw it in snugly. Don't worry that it doesn't engage the rubber seal that was provided with the element.

*A plastic film can be spotted on the end of the electrical cord in **6–22**. Slip this over the electrical connections and hold it with tape—this adds a safety dimension. Note also the green ground wire secured to the handle of the tank with a bolt. Don't omit it. Often, when heating elements "die," they short to ground or neutral. Should this happen and the ground wire is omitted, you could receive a nasty shock instead of the breaker being harmlessly tripped.*

It is necessary that the boiler operate with some pressure. Water from condensation will form in the steam line during operation, so there must be enough pressure to force the water out of the hose. Also, boiling water under pressure increases the temperature of the steam. Every few degrees can help.

A can filled with wheel weights (those small pieces of lead used to balance tires that can be found at your local tire store) used as a safety relief does the job, and it can be conveniently lifted off for filling purposes (**6–25**). But don't forget to save the can's lid. You can solder it back on after the bolt and wheel weights are in place.

Insulation around the tank is a must. It makes for fuel economy and in the summer the tank will not add heat to your shop. Fiberglass was used for the tank shown in this section. Make sure that that foam you use does not melt when it comes into contact with the hot tank.

Place the tank in a plastic container. The plastic container is neat and clean (**6–26**).

Operation and Safety Precautions

The electric heating element has one serious drawback: If the tank cooks dry, the element will self-destruct. Therefore, the element must be immersed in water. Before starting the boiler, check the water level, inserting a small stick through the filler pipe. Starting with about three gallons, at an altitude of 4,000 feet, the boiler (at 1,200 watts) takes about 40 minutes to build a head of steam and consumes about one gallon per hour. *Keeping careful track of time is an important safety technique.*

Remove the filler-pipe cap before starting the boiler. When steam flows freely from the filler pipe, hold the hose in the air to drain any

6-26 and **6-27.** Closeups showing the tank stored in the plastic container.

water trapped in it. Couple the hose to the appropriate fixture, and then install the cap. This ensures that you don't handle a very hot hose.

Caution! If you have to remove the filler-pipe can to check the water level while the boiler is in operation, drape an old bath towel over it, shown in **6–27.** *A significant amount of hot steam will be released, and it could cause some nasty burns. Also, a sudden release of pressure will cause the water in the tank to* *boil violently, often spewing out of the filler pipe. Remove the can very slowly. The towel will insulate your bare hands and prevent steam from blowing into your face or other parts of your body.*

MISCELLANEOUS VENEERING TECHNIQUES

Veneering Moldings

Often the cost of solid, exotic wood for moldings is prohibitive. Sometimes exotic species make very poor solid lumber—satinwood comes to mind. And then, there are those instances where you may want some decorative effect on a molding. In all of these cases, moldings may be veneered—provided, of course, that there is some attention paid to design.

It's a good idea to practice with a heavy piece of paper, planning the best way to attack the project. You will also note that the veneer hammer is going to be impractical. Practice will help you design the type of squeegee—or squeegees—that works best for the operation.

When hammering a molding with hot hide glue, spread the veneer and hammer one edge in a convenient character of the mold (**6–28**). After the edge has set for 15 minutes or so, gently heat the unbonded portion of the veneer to remelt the glue, and then hammer it into the remaining portion of the character. Always work in some cross-grain veneer into the molds you veneer. Usually it's best to place these in a larger character or portion of the molding's design. Sometimes these pieces need to be pre-formed. This can be easily done by band-sawing a piece of scrap to fit the character (seen to the right in **6–28**), placing the moistened pieces to be pre-formed

6-28. Veneering molding with hot hide glue.

between the molding and the band-sawn piece, clamping all of them, and letting them set overnight. You may have to construct a "hammer" to match the curvature of the molding (**6–29**), but the effort is well worth it.

Veneering Turnings

Veneered turnings can also add a special element to any project. Small pieces of veneer laid over any flat spots on a turned component can make for an interesting design. A column veneered with olive ash or Carpathian elm burl can take on the appearance of marble. A mahogany crotch can make a column appear as if it's on fire. The various decorative effects are endless. All are eye-catching, because the eye doesn't expect to encounter these effects on a round piece of wood.

To veneer the convex portion of a turning, you'll need a hammer that fits the diameter of the turning. Prepare a hammer that has a radius about 5 percent greater than the radius of the surface being veneered. Use only 15 degrees of the circumference. If the ham-

6-29. A shop-made hammer used for veneering molding.

6-31. Softening the veneer with an iron.

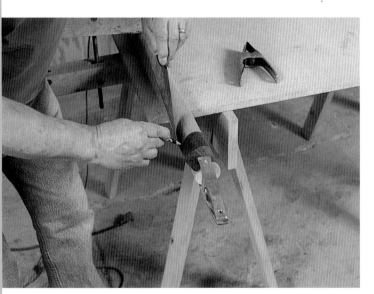

6-30. Using felt paper to locate where to set the veneer.

6-32. Extra-long veneer can be trimmed after the glue is set.

mer has a greater circumference, you won't be exerting any pressure and the extra width will get in the way.

Veneering a simple cylinder requires little effort. Merely spread glue on the cylinder and wrap the veneer around it. Work out the excess glue with the specially prepared hammer, and double-cut the joint. If the glue is left a little thick, it will shrink as it dries, tending to tighten the joint. I have seen some rather impressive puddles of glue under veneer on curved, antique pieces of all sorts.

If the cylinder is not true, rather having a slight bulge—as with some columns—start at the bulge and try to stretch the veneer slightly around the greater surface. Wet the veneer in that area of the bulge and try to stretch the veneer slightly around the greater surface. If the veneer buckles in the areas of lesser diameter, mash it as flat as possible.

If the diameter of the turning varies greatly, it will have to be veneered in pieces. These pieces need not be all of the same species. Some terrific effects are possible. The options are so great that space forbids considering even a few. I will recommend the use of patterns and experimentation. Discover the limitations of the species and turning being used and make necessary adjustments.

Spiral Veneering

Spiral-veneered columns are especially eye-catching. The process is simple and well worth the effort. Once you have determined the width of veneer that will be worked, cut a piece of felt paper to the same width and wrap it around the column in order to determine the pitch of the spiral. Then make a mark to show where to set the veneer (**6–30**). In **6–31**, an iron is being used to soften the veneer and prevent it from splitting. It will be bonded to the column with contact cement. The face of stubborn species should also be moistened. It's always best to work with extra-long veneer if possible and trim it after the glue has had a chance to set for a while (**6–32**).

CHAPTER 7

ADDING A FINISH

When light strikes the surface of a piece of wood, it is reflected in many different directions by the cells and pores. When a clear finish is put over the wood, the pores and cells fill with this clear substance, turning it into tiny lenses and prisms that further diffract the light and even alter its color. With this in mind, all finishing processes should be geared to enhance this property.

In most cases, there is no simple one-step approach to finishing. A system that uses several steps of colors, fillers, glazes, and topcoats—all applied at the proper time in the process—will create a professional finish. Colors of different types and hues can be applied at various stages in the process to produce a wide range of effects (**7–1**). Fillers may be applied over bare wood, after sealing, or both. Topcoats may be full gloss or have a flattening agent mixed into them to obtain the desired sheen without the necessity for rubbing.

The subject of wood finishing can be volume length. It basically consists of patching and sanding the wood that will take the finish, applying the stain or finish that will alter the color of the veneer, and then applying the topcoat. The patching and sanding process and the various products available for finishing are described below.

PATCHING

As you probably well know, the first step in any finishing operation is patching and sanding, and there is a lot of sanding involved. There is no beautifying finishing technique that hides scratches and other defects. More often, the finish magnifies these defects as it magnifies the beauty of the wood.

Often, there are spots such as a slightly open joint or a hole in a burl that need a little patch. Make sure that you create a smooth surface in the finished product. For most patching, nitrocellulose putty is recommended. It's not only the most common product at the paint store, it also serves well in most instances. You may decide to choose the lightest color available, preferring the stain to

7-1. Spraying on a finish.

add color to the patch. If the stain doesn't color it sufficiently, you can add color after the piece is sealed. (It's always easier to make a patch darker than lighter.)

In those areas where the species is likely to fade dramatically—and this will become obvious—create a patch by adding dust produced from the piece you are sanding to some thinned liquid hide glue. Because the particles in the patch are of the same species, they will fade at an equal rate and to the same color, and the transparency of the hide glue will let some iridescence still left in the particles shine through.

SANDING

In veneering, the grain may change due to a border. Figured species often have no set grain direction. In this case, disregard grain direction. To level up different thicknesses of veneers, feel free to use 80-grit sandpaper wrapped around a block of wood (**7–2**). Use a circular motion if it feels good. You will need to cut away quite a bit of material, and cutting

cross-grain cuts much faster than with-the-grain.

There is a definite reason for using the wood block. If your veneer is coarse, open-grained, soft sandpaper will cut away at the grainy areas far more quickly than the harder areas, leaving you with a mess of ripples.

Once you have the surface leveled up, it will be covered with some very ugly 80-grit scratches. Sand these out. Use 120-grit sandpaper to do so. A rule of thumb here is that it takes 10 to 15 passes with the 120-grit sandpaper to remove the scratches left by the 80-grit. (You may have heard or read that sanding with a well-used piece of 80-grit sandpaper will give the same finish as a piece of 120-grit sandpaper. Not true. A few sharp pieces of 80 grit will remain cutting deep scratches. You are not sanding with finer grit. You are sanding with dull 80-grit.)

Now switch to 220-grit. Keep this sandpaper moving in a straight line. By doing this you will know that any curved scratches were left by the circular motion of the 120-grit paper. Keep sanding until these are gone. You

7-2. Sanding with a block wrapped with sandpaper.

could keep going and use 320-grit sandpaper, but scratches from 220-grit paper are not noticeable under most finishes.

Power Sanding

If you are using a belt sander in your veneer work, be careful: One mistaken twist of the wrist or one sudden motion can leave a deep gouge that can be impossible to remove without sanding through the veneer. It takes a lot of practice to use a belt sander skillfully.

If you must use a belt sander, use nothing coarser than 120-grit paper—even for leveling. Support most of the sander's weight and use it very delicately. Actually lift it from the surface after each pass.

If you have a random orbit sander, consider that most of these sanders have a soft pad. This will cause the paper to cut away at the areas of course grain much faster than the areas of harder areas between, as described above. A random orbit sander can be used for one quick pass with 220-grit paper, nothing more.

ALTERING THE COLOR OF VENEER

It may be that you have fallen in love with the grain pattern and texture of a particular veneer species, but are not crazy about the color. Don't fret; the color of wood can be altered, in many cases with only minor work. Altering the color of the veneer to a darker shade, or to a darker shade with a different hue, is probably the easiest. Altering the color to what appears to be a lighter shade can be done easily using dyes. Actually making the wood a lighter shade is more difficult and often compromises the iridescent properties of the wood because pigments or bleach will be required.

No one product or technique should be adopted exclusively. There are so many different species and techniques available that to limit your approach to a single method will mean not taking advantage of the versatility that is so important in wood finishing.

Pigmented Stains

Stains containing pigments are probably the most popular consumer product for altering the color of wood. They are easy to use, and blending the various colors of pigment to achieve a particular hue is also easy. Consumer pigmented stains are usually of the brush-on/wipe-off variety and may be solvent-, oil-, or water-based. With these stains, wood can easily be made darker and actually made lighter through the use of a light-colored pigment. And the pigments usually concentrate in the grain of the wood, enhancing the grain pattern. However, they also can completely destroy the iridescent properties of the wood. Pigments are actually finely ground rocks. Their colors are lightfast (resistant to light), but they are not transparent and do not permit the passage of light. It's like looking at the surface through a film of mud.

Scratches and slightly open joints pick up pigments, so the full "beauty" of these defects is intensified. Also, pigments tend to settle into end grain more than flat grain. Wavy species like maple will appear blotchy.

While pigmented stains are quick and easy to use, there are better ways to go. These methods are discussed below.

Dye Stains

Unlike pigmented stains, dye stains are fully transparent. They alter the color of the wood without affecting its iridescent properties. Unfortunately, they are not as lightfast as pigmented stains, and some fading can be expected through the years. But remember, if you are finishing new wood, it is not lightfast either.

Not as easy to find as pigmented stains, dye stains are supplied in powdered form or dissolved in a number of mediums: water, alcohol, oil, toluene, etc. Many liquid dyes are supplied in concentrated form and should be thinned to the desired strength. It's always best to thin the stain with the same medium as in the concentrate. If this is not possible, compatible thinners may be used. Water stains may be thinned with alcohol—to make them dry faster and minimize the grain-raising tendencies of the water. Alcohol stains may be thinned with lacquer thinner—if you don't have any alcohol on hand. In any event, if you have chosen a poor combination—such as thinning oil dyes with water, particles will form on the bottom of the container.

Dye stains are not quite as easy to blend to produce a particular color as are pigmented stains. This is because the dyes are transparent, so the color of the wood comes more heavily into play. When the dye stain is wet, it will appear to be one color; when it dries, the color changes dramatically. Then, when the topcoats are applied, a third color results. This color is usually very similar to the color of the wet stain, but not always. If that isn't enough, because the dyes are fully transparent, the color will change as the surface is viewed from different angles—as mentioned in "Veneer Presentations" in Chapter 1. Suffice it to say that experiments should be carried out on scraps, and that the experimental pieces should be given topcoats and viewed under a number of light conditions to ensure a critical match.

Dye stains should be sprayed on. Trying to apply these with a brush or by wiping them on with a rag can be very tricky. Because they absorb and dry so quickly, lap marks will become evident—very evident. Spraying does give the advantage of being able to color the wood without being at the mercy of the absorption properties thereof. A specific amount is applied to certain areas of the wood, where it is absorbed. And while dye stains don't cover sanding scratches and slightly open joints, they don't accentuate them either.

For maximum effect, the dyes should be applied in heavy, penetrating coats—almost to the point where the dyes run. This happens quite often when I use dyes, so I keep a rag tucked in my back pocket that I use to quickly blot them.

It is impossible to lighten a particular species with dyes, but it can be made to look lighter. When you want to quickly make new, deep-purple walnut look like old, faded walnut, spray it with bright-orange dye. The bright orange makes the walnut appear lighter. The resultant color will not pass critical examination, but is a quick fix. There is beauty in the process in that if the piece is exposed to light, as the dye color fades, the natural color of the walnut develops. Bright-yellow dye, a dab of orange, and a dab of brown will work the same way in making new oak look like aged oak.

If you opt to use dye stains to finish veneer, practice on scrap instead of your project, and be sure to read the section on glazing stains below, for wood colored with only dyes can be quite stark and will need to be toned down.

Combination Stains

Some consumer wood stains are a combination of dyes and pigments. If you put a stick in a fresh can of this type of stain, you'll find

together. Several layers of thick tape could interfere with the bonding operation.

CUTTING CURVES

Marquetry can consist of simple, straight-line geometrical designs. But in this craft you might find yourself cutting a lot of curves.

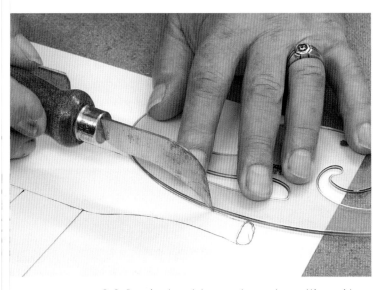

8-2. Drawing templates may be used as cutting guides.

8-3. Knife tipped up to make stabbing cuts on a tight curve.

Cutting Surface

Unlike heavy-duty veneering, in the craft of marquetry you will be making some very fine, precise cuts. You will want the best cutting surface. Poster board works very well. You can trim the sides off department store gift boxes or even use the back of a scratch pad. When your cutting surface becomes somewhat "ratty," throw it away and start afresh.

This can be a tricky freehand, so use some type of aid such as drawing instruments (**8–2**). Just be sure that you don't cut into the aid. Let the blade, not the cutting edge, follow the aid.

At some point, you might find yourself attempting to cut a very tight curve where the knife seems to have little effect. Here use a hobby knife; tip it up and make a series of stabbing cuts (**8–3**). You might have to repeat the process several times, but the technique works well.

You can use a saw to cut very tight curves and intricate patterns. Some veneer suppliers offer tools as well as veneers and you can purchase what is called a "fretsaw" from them. A fretsaw is similar to a coping saw, but it has a deep throat and will accept blank-end jeweler's saw blades (**8–4, upper**). These blades come in a number of widths and are much finer than a coping saw blade—50 teeth per inch or more. They are also far more fragile. Don't be ashamed if you break a couple when starting off. Do some practicing with a #1 blade, which is about the coarsest blade you will want to use in marquetry.

If your project is small, you might want to consider an actual jeweler's saw (**8–4, lower**). The smaller frame is much easier to handle. Be it a fretsaw or jeweler's saw, try to

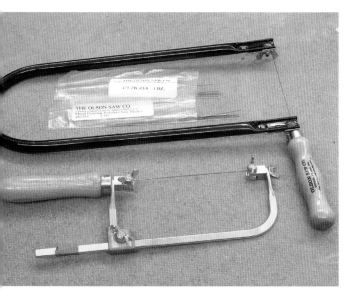

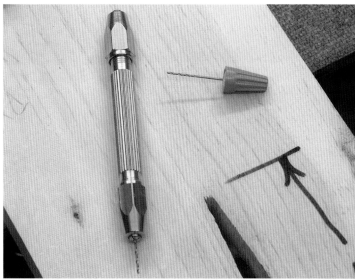

8-4. Two types of saw for veneer. Above: fretsaw. Below: jeweler's saw.

8-6. Hobby drill for making holes for a saw blade.

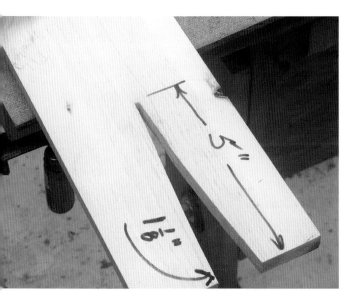

8-5. A bird's mouth for use with a fretsaw.

set your mind to ignore the frame. Concentrate on the handle, the blade, and the work.

Before you begin practicing with your saw, you will have to construct a very simple fixture called a "bird's mouth." Illus. **8–5** shows a bird's mouth with its dimensions written on it. The purpose of this fixture is to support the veneer as it's being cut. Keep the saw blade as close to the crotch of the V shape as possible, to provide maximum support for the veneer. To accomplish this, operate the saw from a comfortable sitting position with your elbow resting on your knee or against your lower ribcage. This will give your arm a point of reference. Move only your elbow and your wrist but slightly. While this may seem a bit uncomfortable, it will save you a fortune in blades.

There will come a time when you will have to cut a character out of the center of a piece of veneer. Have on hand a small drill to bore a hole through which to thread your fretsaw blade. This can be a hobby drill or one that can be made by setting a 1/32-inch drill bit in a wire nut filled with epoxy (**8–6**).

If you have a scroll saw that will accept blank-end saw blades, use them. One challenge here: You should fabricate a new table insert with a very fine blade slot to provide

8-7. Table insert for a scroll saw.

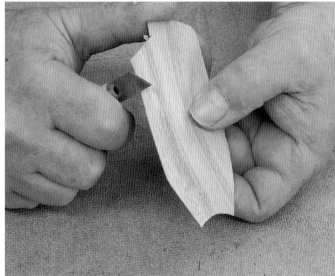

8-9. Whittling an incorrect cut.

8-8. Cutting veneer with a woodcarving tool.

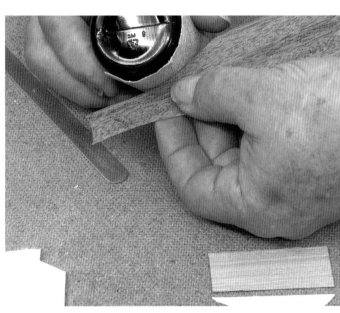

8-10. Correcting a cut using sandpaper.

maximum support for the veneer. The one shown in **8–7** is a piece of acrylic sheet. Also, run your saw at minimum speed to start. Jeweler's saw blades are very fragile and will not mechanically take the punishment of high speeds.

Other tools that can be used to cut curves are woodcarving tools. Gouges cut very accurate curves. In many instances, these tools will tend to chip the veneer if forced to cut into the heart of a sheet. The most effective way to use a carving tool is to rough cut the piece and then refine the cut with a carving tool. Dig in the corner of the tool and then rock it forward along the line in a shearing motion (**8–8**). And, don't forget that skews and chisels may be used for straight cuts in the same manner.

ADJUSTING CUTS

If the cut comes out short, you'll have to try again or use a patch in the finished product—which will look awful. If the cut is a bit long, however, it can be adjusted in a number of ways. You can very carefully whittle or scrape it with the grain using a knife (**8–9**). For an inside curve, you can wrap a piece of sandpaper—nothing coarser than 120-grit—around anything round that will come close to fitting the curve (**8–10**). For outside curves, you can use an emery board (**8–11**) or a stick with sandpaper glued to it. The moral: It's far less time-consuming to cut carefully the first time.

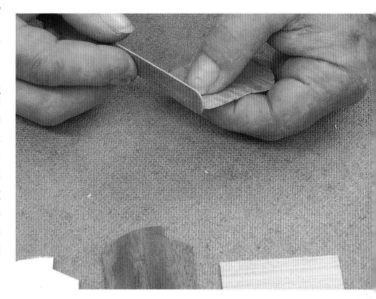

8-11. Correcting a cut using an emery board.

CUTTING TECHNIQUES

There are a number of ways to approach a marquetry project. You might wish to use a particular technique exclusively on your project or use a combination of techniques to fit your needs. Let's investigate the various techniques.

Pattern-Cutting

If you have done stained-glass work, this technique will be familiar. Make a drawing of the project on heavy paper or poster board. Then cut components from the drawing and place them on the veneer for use as cutting templates (**8–12**). Then tape the pieces of veneer together and get them ready for bonding.

This technique can lend itself to some inaccuracy for a piece of artwork. You might not cut the pattern perfectly. Then, using the imperfect pattern piece, you are going to cut an imperfect veneer. Two cuts multiply the error.

Window-Cutting

Let's examine a technique that can be a bit more accurate than pattern-cutting. With this

8-12. Cutting a template from a drawing.

technique, you draw the project on the background. Then cut a window for a particular component. (If you are using a scroll saw to cut the window, have on hand a tiny drill to make a hole in the sheet of veneer to thread the saw blade through.) Next, use this win-

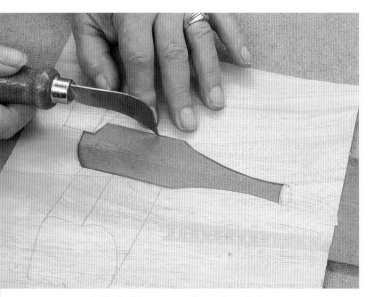

8-13. Cutting veneer through a window.

8-15. Component used as a template to cut a window.

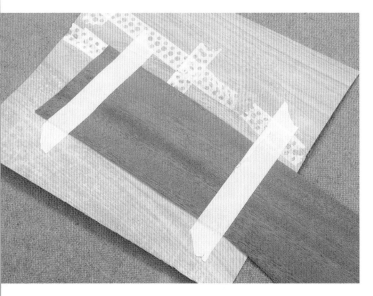

8-14. Masking tape is being used to hold veneer in place.

dow as a template to cut the component from a sheet of veneer (**8–13**). If you feel you can't cut the component without it slipping, tape it to the background (**8–14**).

You can do this backwards, that is, pattern-cut the component and use it as a template to cut a window in the background

(**8–15**). If your project is large, you'll find the latter method much easier.

Multi-Cutting

It stands to reason that if two veneers are stacked and cut at the same time, the one on top will fit into the one on the bottom or the other way around. This is true, but unless you are using two easy-to-cut species it is difficult to do this with a knife. Here is where you can make good use of a fret or scroll saw.

You must remember that a saw removes material. The space left between the two cut components is called a "kerf." The kerf taken by a #3/0 blade is about .005 inch—about half the thickness of a matchbook cover. Now, in assembly a component could shift to one side, leaving that side tight and the other with a gap of .01 inch. To purists that is probably an intolerable inaccuracy. But, there are mass-produced pieces where the background appears to have been cut with a router, then the components bonded therein. Some gaps are wide enough to roll a nickel down. In the

Masking tape will often suffice to hold pieces in register for multi-cutting. If the pieces are quite small and complex, a simple, temporary adhesive called "rubber cement" will come in very handy. It's best to use a thin spread on both surfaces. When you part the pieces, rubbing with a fingertip will cause the cement to ball up, and it can be easily removed. It's best not to leave the pieces bonded with rubber cement for more than a day or two, as that bond can become quite strong as the cement cures. Often it is desirable to use a combination of tape and cement.

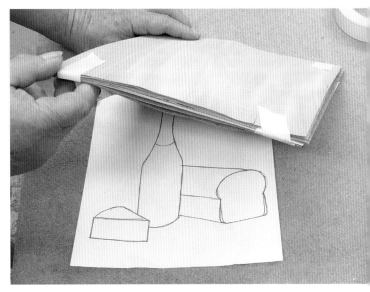

8-16. A pad prepared for cutting.

finishing process, the manufacturer has filled the gaps with clear resin, and from a couple of steps back the gaps are not offensive. You should use a heavy yellow glue spread and press, letting the glue fill the gaps; from one step back, the gaps are barely noticeable.

Pad-Cutting

Pattern-cutting, window-cutting, and even multi-cutting are fine, but handling all of those individual pieces is rather time-consuming. Pad-cutting allows you to cut all of the pieces at once.

With this technique, all of the various species to be used in the project are cut to the same size, stacked, and secured with rubber cement and/or masking tape, forming a pad (**8–16**). Draw the design on the top layer, and then with a fretsaw or scroll saw cut all of the pieces at once. There is one drawback to this technique: it wastes a lot of material. When you have finished assembling the pieces you want, you will have a virtual pile of leftovers (**8–17**). If you can use the leftovers in a contrasting

8-17. Leftovers from pad-cutting.

project, that's well and good. Illus. **8–18** shows an economical way to pad-cut.

There is an alternative. Draw a mirror image of your project on the back of the background and tape pieces of veneer a little bit larger than a particular character only where they are needed (**8–18**). This, of course, will

8-18. Economical tape-up for pad-cutting.

8-19. A finished marquetry project.

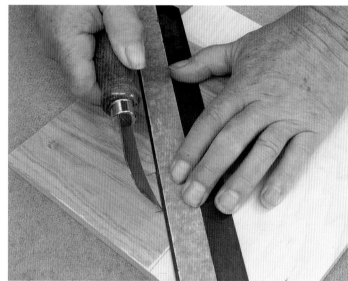

8-20. Cutting for a triangular inlay.

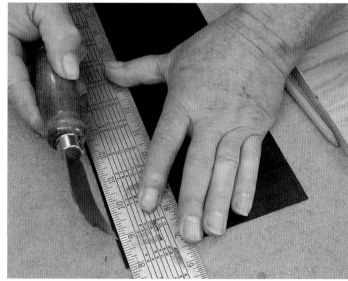

8-21. Cutting a triangular piece for an inlay.

result in a rather lumpy pad. But, with a little thought in layout and care in cutting, it can save you a fortune in veneer.

No matter how you cut, bond, or finish, you should come up with a piece of artwork. The depiction of bread, wine, and cheese in **8–19** is called the "The Stuff of Life."

SPECIAL INLAY TECHNIQUES

There will come a time when you want to execute a design that has one or more components that are seemingly impossible to depict in wood veneer. Don't let that seeming impossibility stop you! Marquetry is a very flexible craft.

One thing that seems to be impossible to depict is fine lines, and in a tape-up that can be true. But wait until the project is bonded. Then mark the location with the help of a straightedge, tip your knife, and make a cut (**8–20**). Turn around and make a diagonal cut on the opposite side. Remove the tiny triangular piece of veneer.

Next, cut a triangular strip of contrasting veneer by again tipping your knife (**8–21**). Glue the strip into the groove and sand it flush with the surface. It's very simple to inlay fine lines.

But say you want a curved line. This is also simple if you have a steady hand and good eyesight. Draw your curved line and cut diagonally along it (**8–22**). Cut diagonally along the other side of the line, again removing a triangular piece. You are not going to be able to cut a triangular piece of veneer to fit any tight curve—perhaps a gentle curve that the strip will bend into, but not a tight curve.

If you insist that your masterpiece be all of wood, you could mix some sanding dust from the contrasting veneer with liquid hide

8-22. Cutting a curved groove for an inlay.

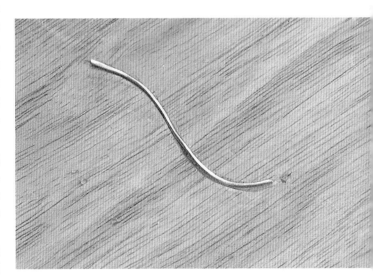

8-23. Inlaying with copper.

glue and fill the cut. But think about metal. Illus. **8–23** shows a piece of 20-gauge copper wire that fit the cut very well. You don't have to use copper. A jewelry supply store can fix you up with silver or gold, and it will have triangular wire. Be creative in this wonderful craft.

8-24. A marquetry project using shading.

SHADING

Before you move on to the projects in Part 2, one more technique should be described. Perhaps you want to depict one piece of veneer lying beneath another of the same species, such as the faux leaves shown in **8–24**. Shading will do this.

Shading is easily accomplished by standing your veneer pieces in an electric fry pan with about 1 inch of sand in the bottom (**8–25**). You will want to do a bit of experimenting here with scraps. The fry pan works best when you set it to 400 degrees, and the time it takes to discolor the wood depends on the species.

8-25. Shading pieces using sand in an electric fry-pan.

PART **2**   PROJECTS

BEFORE YOU BEGIN

Now that you have digested the information on veneers, substrates, bonding, etc., you are ready to work on some projects. The projects in this section start off simply and increase in complexity. They include three basic projects (a box, coasters, and a checkerboard), a lamp, blanket, kidney-shaped desk, dining table, and bombé chest. Mike Burton takes you step by step through his entire veneering process, including the problems he encountered and his solutions. You can adapt the dimensions of each project to suit your particular needs and the veneer you decide to use.

CHAPTER 9

SIMPLE PROJECTS

Now that you digested the information on veneers, substrates, bonding, etc., you should be ready to work on some projects. This chapter contains information on veneering three simple projects: a box, coasters, and a checkerboard.

SIMPLE BOX

Let's start off with something that will use only a small amount of veneer, glue, and ground material while giving you a useful item (**9–1**).

Many hobby and craft suppliers sell plain pine boxes to be adorned with decorative painting, decoupage, etc. Why not adorn one of these with exotic veneer? When you go shopping for a box, select one with a lid that fits the bottom. Also, be sure that it has no rounded corners.

Since I was not able to find a box that fit the above simple criteria, I decided to build my own. I planed a piece of 2³/4-inch wide alder 27 inches long to a ¹/2 inch thickness and then cut a ¹/4-inch square dado down each

9-1. Pine box adorned with veneer.

edge. From this stick, I cut two pieces 8 inches long and two pieces 4 inches long and nailed them together with a tiny bead of glue at each joint. I did pay careful attention as to the placement of the nails, making sure that there was no nail driven ³/4 inch below the top. The reason will become apparent as we go on. And feel free to adapt my dimensions to your own wants and needs.

Once the four sides were nailed together, I cut pieces of 1/4-inch birch-faced MDF for the top and bottom. After putting a tiny bead of glue in the dado, I set the top in place and put a weight on it. After 20 minutes set time, I did likewise with the bottom.

If you have followed my construction details, by now you have probably noticed a 1/4-inch cubical void at all of the corners of your box. Fill this void with auto-body putty. Once the putty has cured, sand all six sides so that no component stands proud of any other. On display in **9–2** is my finished and sanded masterpiece. I have shaded the auto body fills with a pencil for your viewing pleasure, as well as put in the leftover piece of the dadoed stick.

Next, select a slice of your favorite veneer and mark on it with chalk the areas you intend to take cuts for the sides and top. I decided on a slice of East Indian rosewood. This slice had a light area along one edge, and I felt that this would work well for the bottom of the sides. The sides would then color-flow into a very dark area I chose for the top. In marking, leave yourself an extra 1/2 inch for trimming.

Spread both veneer and the edges of your box with two thinned coats of contact cement (about 10 percent thinner), allowing complete drying between coats. Then, with the veneer setting flat on your bench, set one side of your box on the veneer, leaving a little to trim all around. Press the box down firmly and then trim by setting your veneer saw flat against the box (**9–3**).

Once the veneer is trimmed, roll or rub down it firmly and thoroughly. In lieu of a roller or veneer hammer, you can use a small scrap of wood with any of the sharp edges removed (**9–4**). Once the veneer is rubbed

9-2. The box ready for veneering.

down, feel the edges. If any stand proud, smooth them flush with a shooting block. Move the block from the veneer toward the box. Moving in the opposite direction could pull the veneer loose or damage the surface. If the shooting has spread significant dust to the contact on an opposing side, give that side another light coat of contact and let it dry. Repeat the process with all sides and the top.

Once the veneer is all in place and sanded, you must cut off the lid. I chose my band saw for the operation, it being very safe for a small box. I set the fence to 3/4-inch to blade center (**9–5**). The operation can also be preformed on a table saw making four passes. Just be sure that you don't let the blade protrude more than 1/8 inch more than necessary to cut thorough the sides.

Once the lid is parted you can use your shooting block to remove saw marks from both the bottom and lid. Then resaw some 1/8-inch-thick material wide enough to stand 1/8-inch proud of the bottom of the box and as long as necessary to line the sides of the bottom. Fit this into the bottom. This will serve

9-3. Trimming veneer bonded to the box end.

9-5. Cutting the lid from its bottom.

9-4. Firmly bonding veneer.

9-6. Installing the lid locator.

as a lid locator (**9–6**). Feel free to miter the corners, and if you fit it snug enough, you won't have to glue it in.

A little sandpaper to knock off the sharp edges of the lid locator and the edges where the lid was parted and you are ready for a finish. I chose Danish oil for my finish.

COASTERS

Let's work a very simple marquetry project. How about a set of coasters to prevent your guest's sweating beverage glasses from spoiling the finish on your end tables and coffee table (**9–7**)?

Secure two or more species of your favorite veneer and some small pieces of ¼-inch plywood or MDF that are 4½-inches square or larger. A strip 4½ inches wide will be preferable. You'll see why as the project progresses.

On a piece of poster board or the back of a scratch pad, draw a 3½-inch circle. Divide one half the circumference into four parts. Cut from your drawing a one-fourth section to use as a pattern for the segment of an octagon (**9–8**) (if you trust a protractor to construct the segment, go for it). Using this pattern, mark and cut pieces of each species. And, don't be so vain as not to use aids to guide your cuts (**9–9**). Also, you will find that the corners at the periphery of the circle are quite fragile. Take the time to put some tape over these areas. I started reinforcing with perforated tape. When I discovered that the tiny spot I wanted to reinforce often fell under a perforation, I switched to solid tape.

If you have a scroll saw, don't hesitate to stack four or five layers secured with rubber cement (as described in Chapter 8) and cut them all at once. If the straight cuts made with the scroll saw are a bit wavy, shoot them while they are still secured with the rubber cement. Don't worry about shooting the curved edge of the section just yet.

It's time to tape all of these little pieces together and get them ready for bonding. Hold on now; don't rush through his process. The assembly will be frustrating and, you'll not be pleased with the finished product. Take time to come up with something other than your fingers to hold the tiny pieces in place. I let my cutting surface hang over the bench a bit while using nothing more than a couple of clothespins to hold the pieces in place (**9–10**).

9-7. Coasters.

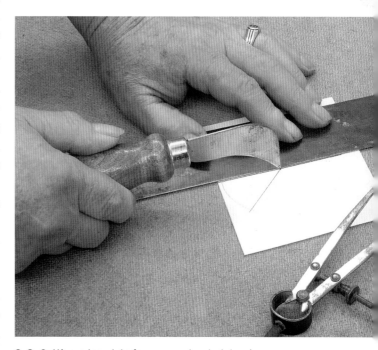

9-8. Cutting a template from a constructed drawing.

9-9. Cutting components from reinforced veneer.

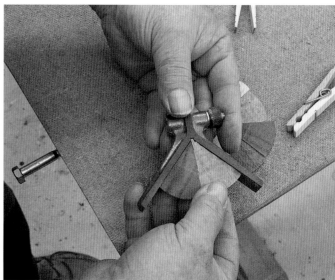

9-11. Checking the assembled components for square.

9-10. Assembling the components.

9-12. Checking halves for a straight taping joint.

Tape only two pieces together at one time to make up the four quadrants of the circle. Line up the curved outer edge and let the points fall where they will. These quadrants should be square. Check each (**9–11**). If any are out of square, shoot them. Then tape two quadrants together. These should form a straight line (**9–12**). If they don't, resort to that shooting block again. Once the halves are straight, tape the circle together.

The reason for all of this checking and shooting is that the cumulative error of eight pieces can be devastating in the finished product. Even a small error in the four quadrants can be difficult to deal with. And, of course, you want the two halves to fit well.

Now, look at the periphery of the circle to see that it is reasonably round. Any error will be where the two halves are joined. Smooth any error out with your trusty shooting block. You're not trying to form a perfect circle, just something that looks round; and you don't want a unaligned piece to show in the periphery.

At this point, you could bond the taped-up pieces to ¼-inch material and pat yourself on the back as the glue dries, but wouldn't this circle look better with a border? Don't answer! Just secure a strip of veneer a minimum of 3 inches wide. Place this beneath the circle and use that circle as a template to cut your border (**9–13**). Cut enough from the strip of veneer to make a border of at least ½ inch. The border won't be that wide in the finished product, but a piece of end-grain veneer much narrower will be quite difficult to handle.

Use your straightedge placed through the center of the circle to cut the border joint (**9–14**). For the next two quadrants, one border joint will be part of the template, and for the last quadrant, both joints will be part of the template.

Once all of border pieces are taped in place, you are ready to bond. You could use contact cement. I chose to use yellow glue and a press. I spread the glue with a plastic laminate sample with notches filed in it as a spreader "trowel." As for the press, nothing high-tech was used here. One clamp and a couple pieces of coated particleboard served very well. As shown in **9–15**, I bonded my coasters to a strip rather than individual pieces of ground. The coasters will be much easier to sand on the strip than individually.

If you use yellow glue, allow about one

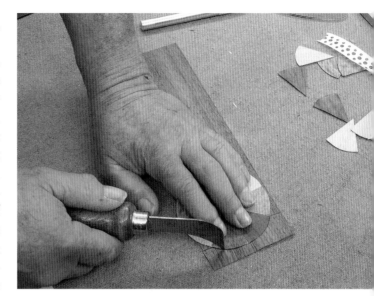

9-13. Cutting a border using the project as a template.

9-14. Cutting a border joint.

hour press time. Then allow overnight drying before removing the tape. Because the taped areas were small, I sanded the tape off using a belt sander with 120-grit paper.

With a pencil compass, draw a circle on each coaster to leave a border of about ¼ inch. Make a trip to your band saw, scroll saw, jig-

9-15. Pressing the project.

9-16. Cutting project pieces from an oversized ground.

saw or what-have-you. Cut out the coasters (**9–16**), sand the saw marks from the edge, and the coasters are ready for a finish.

I chose a salad bowl finish for my coasters. This tung oil product is very resistant to water and to alcohol.

CHECKERBOARD

Let's try another project consuming a minimum of material and supplies. How about a checkerboard (**9–17**)? We'll even do it the easy way and bond with contact cement. You might think this a frivolous project, but there is a bit more precision involved than you might originally think.

To start with, you will need two contrasting veneers at least 8½ inches wide and 17 inches long (I chose tamo and walnut butt). These will be cut into 2-inch strips. There is precision required here.

Making a checkerboard is something like laying floor tile. If you have laid floor tile and found yourself running off about ⅛ inch in the first six rows, you'll understand the importance of precise cutting and fitting.

To aid in this precision, clamp a straight board to your bench. After trimming and shooting one edge of the veneer, butt it against the board. Then lay a 2-inch-wide straight-edge over the veneer and cut (**9–18**). Shoot the edge of the strip you just cut and the edge of the stock and repeat the process until you have four strips of each species. Now hold all eight strips on edge and tap them, as you would when straightening a number of papers (**9–19**). This is a very important step.

If the strips are all exactly the same width, you are truly blessed. My stack was not as perfect as I would have liked, so I ripped two pieces of ¼-inch plywood to 1¹⁵⁄₁₆ inch wide and clamped the veneer strips between the plywood. A couple passes with a shooting block set my mind at ease (**9–20**).

Once you are satisfied that the strips are all of equal width, tape them together (**9–21**). Then trim the tape-up square, go back to your straight board and straightedge, and cut strips of the tape-up (**9–22**), shooting as you go like before. It's a good idea to number the pieces as you cut them from the tape-up. It is quite possible that the sides of your tape-up are not exactly parallel (mine varied by about ³⁄₃₂ inch). If you put the strips back together the

9-17. Checkerboard project.

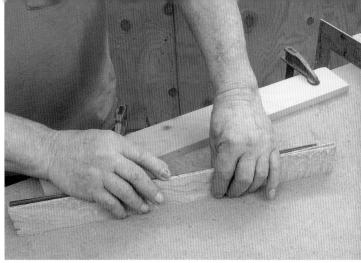

9-19. Checking strips for consistency.

9-18. To make this checkerboard project, the strips of veneer has to be precisely cut.

9-20. Using a shooting board to adjust strips of different widths.

way you took them apart—just reversing the pattern—your finished piece might be a bit out of square, but the squares will line up much better. Again, check to see that they are all the same width, and make adjustments as necessary.

Now tape these strips together. If you have to stop in the middle of the operation, place the tape-up between two pieces of 3/4-inch material and put a weight on it. This will prevent the drying tape from pulling it into a cup. Even once the operation is complete, it's not a bad idea to warm the tape-up with your iron and let it cool between weights. This will make it much flatter and easier to handle.

In between all of this cutting, shooting, and taping, take a break and prepare your ground. This could be as simple as a piece of 1/4-inch material. I chose a piece if 3/4-inch birch plywood which I edge-banded with

9-21. Taping up the strips.

9-23. Spreading contact cement on the ground and tape-up.

9-22. Precisely cutting the tape-up.

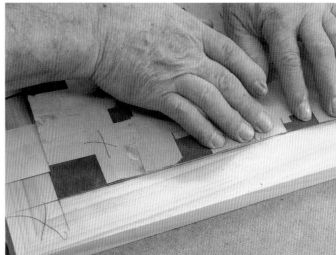

9-24. Gently setting the tape-up in the contact cement.

poplar, because I intended to run a decorative shape around my checkerboard. The entire ground will provide for a 1³/4-inch border around the checkerboard.

Now that you have the checkerboard taped, run a shooting block all round. You might find that after all sides are straightened the tape-up is slightly out of square. As such, I recommend you mark your ground as to the exact location you will be bonding the tape-up, dividing any out of square condition equally. Be sure to mark one corner for setting.

Once you have the marks made, spread the contact cement (**9–23**). I recommend two coats thinned about 10 percent with acetone or lacquer thinner, allowing both coats to dry completely. While you're waiting, select a piece of veneer to use as a border and spread it. You'll need a piece a minimum of 5 inches wide and 36 inches long.

When the glue is thoroughly dry, place your slip-sticks on the ground. What's a slip-stick? In the instructions on many contact cement containers, the manufacturer recommends that you use heavy paper to hold the spread surfaces apart until the pieces are properly positioned. Disregard this. The contact cement can stick to the paper, especially if you're working in a rather warm shop. Use something more substantial.

I prefer strips of plastic laminate two to three inches wide. Even strips of wood an inch or more wide and about ³/₃₂ inch thick will suffice. Make sure there are no slivers or wood whiskers on the sticks. A coat of paste wax will make them even more resistant to sticking—just make sure the wax is completely dry before using the sticks. Be it laminate or wood strips, should they stick, a tap on the side with a hammer will usually free them.

Now, with the slip-sticks in place, set your tape up on the ground and go to the corner you made your set mark on. When you have the tape-up perfectly positioned, with light pressure bring the two surfaces together at the corner. Check the other three corners. If all is well, bring one edge of the tape-up gently into contact (**9–24**). Check the opposite corners. If for some reason the tape-up is out of alignment don't panic, and don't try to force it into alignment. Prepare a small container of acetone or lacquer thinner—a capful is probably all you'll need.

Remove the slip-sticks while holding the unbonded portion of tape-up away from the ground. Turn the ground on edge and dribble the solvent into the bonded area. The bond will break quite easily. Let everything dry and try again. Nothing is forever here. Even if you have rolled down the area, the tape-up will release, though it will take more solvent and more patience.

Once you are convinced that all is in position, begin removing the slip-sticks and smoothing the tape-up with your hands (**9–25**). Once all of the sticks have been removed, break out that roller and begin to

apply some heavy pressure. As I rolled down my tape-up, I noticed several joints that seemed to be buckling—probably because of excess contact cement getting between the veneers. My roller had little effect on these, so I broke out a heavy hammer I use for blacksmithing. The narrow hammerhead concentrated far more pressure than the roller.

9-25. Withdrawing the slip-sticks.

9-26. Using very heavy pressure to put down standing seams.

Putting all the weight I could muster behind the hammer, the joints went down (**9–26**).

Are you ready for the border? I took several end cuts from my strip of border veneer at about a 20-degree angle. I didn't want to use plain 90-degree end grain and I didn't want to use plain strips. Give my way a try.

Cut eight end-grain pieces from your border veneer stock at about 20 degrees and long enough to accommodate your border. Then cut eight with the grain angle running in the opposite direction. Keep them in separate piles.

From one pile, take a piece and trim the edge square. Place this square end in the center of the checkerboard. (As shown in **9–27**, I removed some tape so I could find the center.) After it's positioned, roll it down. Next, take a piece from the opposite pile and trim its edge square to mate with the piece you just put down. Without setting it firmly in the contact cement, check to see that you have a good joint. If the fit is not good, do a little shooting. But if the error is only ¹⁄₆₄ inch or so, don't worry about it. The next step will fix it.

Set an object of some type across the border glue about one inch from the joint. I chose a ¹⁄₈-inch drill bit for the occasion. Lightly set the joint, set the area away from the joint, and roll it down (**9–28**). Now, withdraw the drill bit and roll down the buckle in the veneer working parallel to the joint. This little trick places substantial pressure at the joint area and will close some rather impressive gaps.

Install the next piece of border but place a plastic laminate sample or a piece of posterboard under it at the corner to keep veneer from sticking in that area (**9–29**). Now install the border pieces from the other side and double-cut the miter cut at the corner (**9–30**). Withdraw the plastic sample and set one side of the border. Then using the

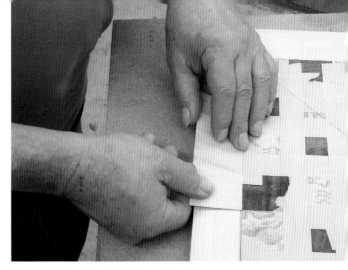

9-27. Installing the first piece of border.

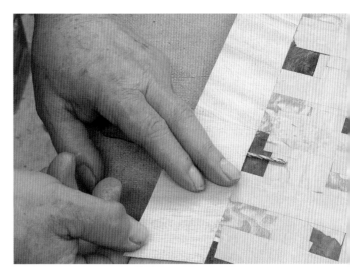

9-28. Installing the second piece of border using a compression joint.

drill bit to buckle the other side, set it and roll down both pieces at the corner. Once the entire border is installed, turn the project over and trim off any veneer that is hanging over (**9–31**).

Once you turn the project back over, you will notice all of that wonderful tape that you worked so hard installing. It now has to come off. You could dig out your trusty belt sander and sand it off, but if you are not well practiced in the use of a belt sander, I don't recommend it. Instead, dig out a small paintbrush and a cup of water. Use the brush to wet only the tape,

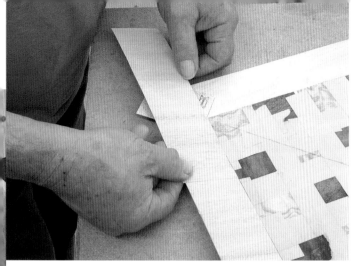

9-29. Installing the second piece of border with a piece of plastic laminate beneath.

9-31. Trimming border excess.

9-30. Double-cutting the corner joint.

9-32. Removing tape using water.

not the veneer. Keep going over the project, wetting the tape. Be patient. It could take ten minutes or more for the water to soften the glue in the tape. Once the glue is softened, the tape peels right off (**9–32**).

Once the tape is removed, allow several hours or overnight drying before sanding. You are bound to have dribbled some water on the veneer, and these areas will swell up. If you sand too soon when these areas dry, there will be shallow spots in your project. Use caution sanding! If you have chosen a coarse-grained veneer such as the tamo I

used, don't even consider using a random orbit sander with a soft pad. It will cut away at the grainy areas far more quickly than the hard areas, leaving a wavy mess. Rather use a block with sandpaper wrapped around it or, if you are skilled with a belt sander, use it—nothing coarser than 120-grit paper. Finish up with a good rubdown of 220-grit and you are ready for any decorative edge and finishing.

I chose to give my project a transparent coat of light golden oak stain—to accentuate the tamo—and then top-coated with lacquer.

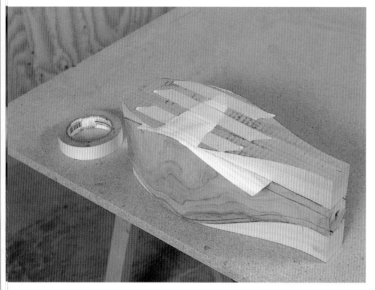

10-11. The pieces of the caul have been taped together.

10-13. Smoothing the cut on the veneered block.

10-12. A piece of carpet between the caul and veneer ensures a good fit.

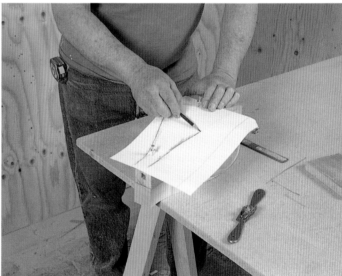

10-14. Transferring the shape to a sheet of paper.

FINAL PROCEDURES

After allowing the assembly to dry overnight again, I trimmed the last two pieces and sketched a line down one edge of the veneered block. That line tapered from the center of the bulge to one corner of an octagon I had laid out on the top. I then cut along this line with a spokeshave, smoothing the cut with a rasp (**10–13**). (You didn't think this was going to be a simple, four-sided lamp, did you? The lamp starts out square and becomes octagonal.)

10-15. Marking the sides.

Once I was satisfied with the cut, I used the side of a pencil to transfer its shape to a piece of paper (**10–14**). After cutting the paper, I used it as a pattern to mark the other sides (**10–15**). I installed the block in a fixture and shaped it with a spokeshave and rasp, turning the top end into an octagon. Then I spread glue on the bare surfaces, preparing them for veneer using the dry-glue process.

After bonding strips of contrasting veneer, I carefully trimmed the excess using my veneer saw—the one sharpened like a knife (**10–16**). In any place where the veneer saw had a tendency to leave the veneer long, I let it do so and finished the job using a curved stick with sandpaper glued to it (**10–17**).

10-16. Trimming the excess.

10-17. Finishing the trimming using a curved stick with sandpaper.

BASE

To accurately cut the veneer for the base—which will be bonded with dry glue—I first made a pattern for the pieces (**10–18**), referencing the bottom of the pattern to the bottom edge of the block.

Using the 45-degree lines on my paper cutter to check the accuracy of the pattern's marks, I cut the veneer (**10–19**), leaving the pencil line on the stock so that the stock would be slightly long. If you don't have a paper cutter, feel free to use a try square and knife or saw.

I bonded the veneer by setting it with the bottom edge and gently rolling it over the curve (**10–20**). Then I trimmed the slight excess on the curved edge flush with the sandpaper-covered stick (**10–21**). The opposing side was worked in the same manner.

To fill in the remaining sides, I cut pieces that had a little excess width at the bottom. I then began bonding these pieces on the top of the block, making sure that the miter cuts fit perfectly (**10–22**). After trimming the bottom edge and a little sanding, I wet one corner with lacquer thinner and took a photo of it to evaluate how it would look under a finish (**10–23**).

Prior to a little sanding, I drilled a hole in the base for the cord and fastened it to the body with drywall screws. After the lamp's journey through the paint shop for clear coats, I installed the electrical fixtures and added a shade.

10-18. Referencing the bottom of the pattern with the bottom of the block, in preparation for making patterns for the base.

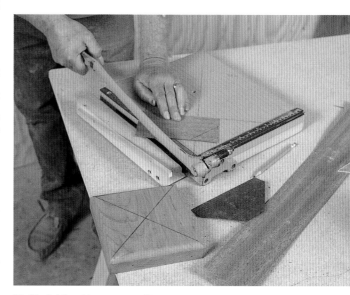

10-19. Cutting the veneer with a paper cutter.

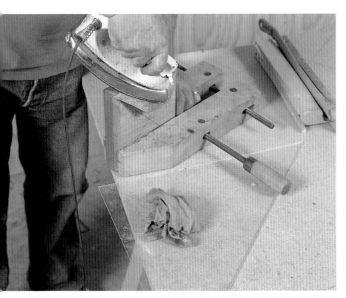

10-20. Bonding the veneer to the base.

10-22. Bonding the opposite sides.

10-21. Trimming the excess of the curved edge.

10-23. The finished base.

CHAPTER 11

VENEERED BLANKET CHEST

Boxes of all sizes and shapes are fun things to veneer. Fun, that is, if the veneer itself is not difficult to work with. In the case of this blanket chest (**11–1** and **11–2**), my client selected lacewood from my box of veneer samples. Lacewood is beautiful, but it is very inconsistent in thickness. This commission was going to require the hot

11-1 and 11-2 (following page). The carcass for this blanket chest is made with pecan plywood, the outside is veneered with lacewood, and cedar makes up the lining. It has a simple, removable cover.

11-2. Note the diamond match for the lacewood and the rounded edges.

11-3. Taping the cedar pieces together for extra length.

persuade my client to select a blanket chest with dimensions that would conform to a pile of pecan plywood leftovers I had stored for some time. She indicated that she didn't want any metal lid supports inside the chest to snag blankets and that no hinges should show, and agreed to a simple removable cover. She also wanted a diamond match for the lacewood and rounded edges.

VENEER LAYOUT AND TAPING

As if having to veneer the outside of the chest with lacewood wasn't bad enough, the cedar I ordered for the lining came in short pieces. Had I used them vertically, there would have been too much waste. The alternative was to trim the ends and tape them into longer lengths (**11-3**). After taping several short pieces together, I cut the appropriate length for the inside of the chest, trimmed the edges,

press in conjunction with urea-formaldehyde glue to make up for the inconsistencies.

There were a couple of things about the project that appealed to me. I did manage to

11-4. Taping cedar pieces together to form the inside of the chest.

11-5. Using a linoleum knife to tear tape.

11-6. Making a chalk mark on the edge of lacewood piece veneer.

11-7. Smoothing the veneer edges. The workbench contains layout lines, and will be used for the front and back of the chest.

and taped them together to provide the needed width (**11–4**). As indicated in **11–5**, a linoleum knife makes a handy straightedge for tearing tape. As also shown in **11–5**, I had to employ lots of pins and any handy weights to hold the cedar flat.

After unpacking the lacewood, the first step was to make my squiggle chalk mark on one edge so that I would keep all cuts running in the proper direction (**11–6**). I did notice some iridescence variation from one side of the sheet to the other, but if a cut of this veneer is turned around or over, the results are devastating as the light-reflecting properties will be very different.

After cutting a number of lengths about an inch longer than needed, to form a shorter diamond, I noted that the edges of the veneer were almost clean enough to make a good joint. A couple of passes with an abrasive shooting block made them perfect (**11–7**). As shown in **11–8** and some of the following photos, there are some layout lines on my "workbench." This workbench will be cut in

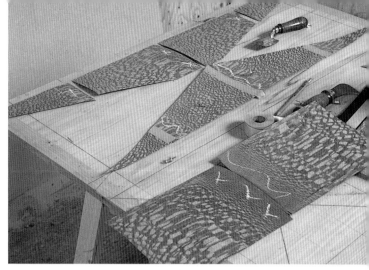

11-9. Forming the second diamond with the waste pieces from the first.

11-10. Using a household iron to set the tape on the waste pieces.

11-8. Cutting the first diamond.

half and used for the front and back of the chest, thus, the alder facing down the center.

Once the pieces were taped together, I cut the first diamond using the layout lines on the bench (**11–8**). The waste pieces were then turned over and placed to form the second diamond. Note the Xs on the waste pieces in **11–9**. These are on the underside of the squiggle line. Theoretically, this should give both of these diamonds similar light-reflecting characteristics. In **11–11**, it looks as if this is to

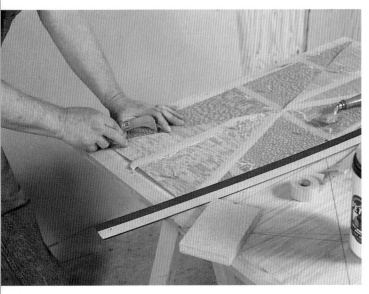

11-11. Marking the longer diamonds for final trimming.

11-12. Another chalk line is made on the lacewood to ensure that the proper direction is followed.

11-13. Using perforated tape to join two pieces.

11-14. Judging proper match from light reflections.

be the case, but only after bonding and finishing will we know for sure.

The waste was then taped and trimmed to size. As shown in **11–10**, an iron was used to firmly set the tape. After the longer diamonds were taped, they were slid under the shorter ones, and marked for final trimming with the point of a linoleum knife (**11–11**). (No I'm not cutting with that knife; I'm only making a very fine and accurate mark.) Once the diamonds were joined, the panel was complete for now. The periphery would be trimmed after bonding.

As I cut further into the sheet of lacewood, it became necessary to trim quite a bit off one edge to maintain a good pattern match. But before trimming, I made another squiggle chalk line so that I wouldn't loose directions (**11–12**).

Progressing even farther, I started putting more pieces of leftover scrap together. In some cases, I didn't know what side would be face up, so I resorted to perforated tape for the joints (**11–13**). This tape is not as strong as the solid type, but it can be left in place even if it winds up in the glue line.

By the time I got to taping up the last small diamonds from the ends of the chest, I was picking up pieces from the floor. Most of these were devoid of chalk marks, but judging from the curl and holding them to the light, I was able to keep the reflections in order (**11–14**).

PRESSING THE VENEER

After the cutting, fitting, and taping, I was relieved to arrive at the relatively fast-moving part of the operation. I chose urea-formaldehyde for this project because of the texture of the lacewood. This glue would fill the irregu-

11-15. Mixing urea-formaldehyde to be used in bonding the veneer.

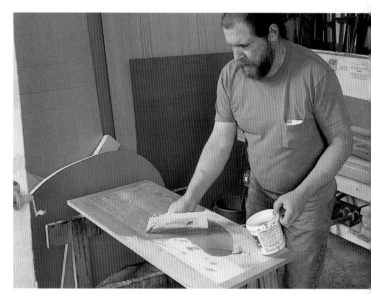

11-16. Spreading the glue.

larities in the veneer and produce a much smoother surface than any other method I could think of. I mixed enough glue to bond the first panel (**11–15**). (I always save empty glue containers and other plastic containers for mixing glue. Those I don't wash out, but let the glue dry in them. Usually some distorting of the container will free the dried glue, and the container can be used again.) For the lacewood, I wanted a slightly thicker glue, so I added glue to water in the proportions of one cup glue to one-third cup water. After mixing thoroughly, I added a dab more water—about one-sixth of a cup.

I then spread the glue with a notched trowel held at a 45-degree angle, being very careful to see that the glue was spread all the way to the edges (**11–16**). After making several final passes with the trowel, I set the taped cedar in place and secured it with masking tape on each corner to keep it in position (**11–17**).

Turning the panel over, I placed the diamond on it and reduced the thickness of the tape in the center with a sanding block (**11–18**)—there were about five thicknesses of tape there. Then I prepared the face of the panel by running some gummed paper painter's tape around the area to which the lacewood would be bonded, placing the tape so glue couldn't reach more than 1/4 inch beyond the area (**11–19**). This is to prevent glue squeeze-out from sticking to the substrate in the border area. The border will be applied with dry glue after the chest's assembly, and cleaning of the urea-formaldehyde squeeze-out could become a nightmare.

With the painter's tape in place, I set the veneers in position using the diagonal layout lines I had transferred to the painter's tape. Then I drew a few more lines and set marks around the veneers that were unlikely to be covered with glue.

After spreading the glue, I quickly replaced the veneers, securing them with masking tape as I did the cedar on the back side.

The press had been closed, and the heater running for about an hour, so the table as well as the aluminum plate were quite hot. I set the panel into the press and, after installing the spanners and the clamps, I made several passes over all the clamps, pulling them down with equal torque.

As a final step, I placed a dab of fresh glue on the edge of the aluminum plate. This would tell me when the glue was cured.

That curing didn't take long. After ten minutes, I could not longer dent the dab of glue with my fingernail. I waited another five minutes before opening the press, because the cedar on the underside of the panel was not exposed to as much heat as the lacewood directly beneath the aluminum plate.

When I opened the press, I noted that the squeeze-out from the cedar side was not rock-hard, so I flipped the panel over and closed the press again. This time, I only installed a few clamps, and these were not firmly pulled down. I wanted only to expose the cedar side to a higher temperature of the aluminum plate.

Five minutes after flipping the panel, I probed at the squeeze-out with a screwdriver. It was rock-hard.

The front, back, top, and ends were all pressed singly in the same manner. As for the bottom, I only bonded the cedar, using no veneer on the other side. I wanted to see just how much the cedar would pull the panel. The glue had grabbed and the moisture had left the panel so quickly that the pull was slight. It only bowed the panel about 1/8 inch over its length. This slight bow could be easily removed when fastening the bottom in place.

After taking the warm panel from the press, I quickly removed the masking tape by pulling it back over itself (**11–20**). The press had done a good job of firmly seating the tape and I didn't want to take the chance of pulling off the surface of the veneer. Had I waited for the tape to cool, this would have been a likely situation—if I could remove the tape at all.

11-17. Adding masking tape to the corners of the cedar panel.

11-19. Running tape around the face of the panel.

11-18. Using a sanding block to reduce the thickness of the tape.

11-20. Removing the masking tape from the panel.

11-21. Trimming the outer edges of the diamonds.

11-23. Using a scraper to level the substrate in the trimmed area.

11-22. A closeup of the router and guides used.

11-24. Assembling the chest with drywall screws and glue. A groove has been cut in the top edge of the pieces to accept the lid.

As the panels were removed from the press, I piled them on sawhorses with stickers between them, allowing the moisture to leave the panel. As I stacked the panels, I noted that the painter's tape did its job well. Squeeze-out from the veneer flowed over the surface of the tape rather than under it.

After several days, I removed the painter's tape in preparation to trim the diamond edges. Removing the tape—and scraping squeeze-out from the edges—was a project that required safety glasses. The rock-hard blobs of glue shattered and flew from the paper as it was pulled from the panel, and pieces of the squeeze-out were propelled from the edge of the scraper with considerable velocity.

Using a router, $3/4$-inch straight cutter, and a guide, I then trimmed the outer edge of the diamonds (**11–21** and **11–22**), setting the router to a depth that would just cut through the veneer. In any places where the router didn't cut quite deep enough—or cut too deeply—a scraper finished the job (**11–23**). This was a good test for the press, for the difference between "too deep" and "not quite deep enough" was only a couple of thousandths of an inch.

Before assembly, I removed all the tape and did some preliminary sanding on the lacewood.

CHEST ASSEMBLY

After a trip to the table saw to cut the necessary rabbets, I assembled the chest with drywall screws and glue. Illus. **11–24** shows the $1/4$-inch groove cut in the top edge of the pieces. A router and slotting cutter were also used to cut a matching groove in the edge of the pieces for the lid. After assembling the

11-25. Using nails to assemble the lid.

11-26. Spreading glue for the borders.

chest, I installed a spline in the groove and assembled the lid with nails (**11–25**). The spline would hold the lid in register and provide a seal.

I will confess that I had a difficult time prying the lid off, but then thinned the exposed portion of the spline with a scraper so that the lid could be lifted off easily. I was lucky; the lid could be replaced in either of its possible configurations—either with its front against the front or its back against the front.

I then rounded the edges with a router. I

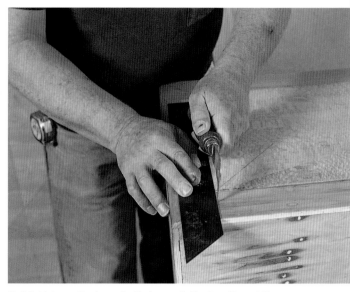

11-29. Using a linoleum knife to mark the location of the field.

11-27. Using a file to remove glue and dust particles from the edge of the veneer.

11-30. Cutting the miter joint.

11-28. Marking the miter joints on the border corner.

11-31. Ironing the border over the rounded edge.

(11–29); these lines were to be used for cutting the joint between the border and field.

After ironing a piece of border on the end of the chest, I trimmed the corner joints using the lines that were carried onto the field as guides (11–30). Then I wet the piece and continued carefully ironing it over the rounded edge, stopping about 1½ inches short of the joint on the other side (11–31).

After rolling the chest over, I clipped the ends of the cut so that I could see the marks made previously with the tip of the linoleum knife. Positioning the straightedge on the marks, I cut the joint using my modified veneer saw. Illus. 11–32 shows a piece of laminate backing sheet under the unbonded veneer to prevent the saw from damaging the edge of the lacewood.

I wouldn't want you to think that all of this work went without incident. Ironing down one piece of border, I noticed that it overlapped the lacewood for about an inch at the end. To force it into place, I held a block of wood against the edge of the veneer and

made a ½-inch radius around the top and a ⅜-inch radius down the sides. While spreading the glue for the borders, I was glad that I'd invested in a good brush (11–26). Cutting that line along the already installed veneer would have been impossible with a cheap one.

After the glue was dry, I went around the edges of the lacewood with the edge of a file (11–27). This was to remove dust particles that might have settled near the joint and also to thin out any glue that might have collected in a puddle along the edges of the lacewood.

Next, I marked the location of the joints at the corner of the border, carrying the line onto the field (11–28). These joints were not quite at a 45-degree angle. Rather, the line extended from the corner of the field to a point where the round in the edge started. I didn't want the tip of the top and bottom border pieces to wrap around the curve. You'll see how it works in the following photos.

On the face and back of the chest, I held a straightedge against the field and marked its location with the tip of a linoleum knife

11-32. A closeup of the cut joint. A piece of plastic laminate is being used under the unbonded veneer to prevent the veneer saw from damaging it.

11-33. Using a mallet to force a piece of border into place.

11-35. Using an iron to force down the buckle near a joint.

11-34. Using a rod to buckle the veneer near a joint.

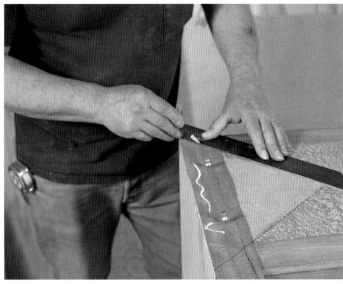

11-36. Cutting the final miter joints.

tapped the block gently with a mallet (**11–33**). Fortunately, the veneer was not completely bonded near the joint. The blow did crack the veneer, but once the errant edge was in place, the warm iron forced the crack back together.

I did try to cut the joints slightly long, but in one instance I left the piece so long that I had to slide a rod under the veneer to buckle it enough to get the edges together (**11–34**). Illus. **11–35** gives an idea of how large a buckle can be forced down.

I also cut one joint a little short—about half the thickness of a utility-knife blade. That I resolved to fix with a little patching putty. Putty is very difficult to detect when two contrasting woods meet.

After rounding these corner pieces, the straight pieces were easy. I merely pinned a rough-cut piece of border in place and marked the joints using the lines on the field as a guide (**11–36**). If the miter joints didn't fit perfectly, I adjusted them with a sanding block. And after the adjustments, if the whole cut came up a little short, I trimmed a little off the edge that met the lacewood.

The pieces of veneer on hand were once inch short of making the long border cuts, so I put a keystone in the center of the piece, to make up a design that would allow me to use the shorter pieces (**11–37**).

Even with the few minor challenges, the border work on the chest went well, and the pieces at the corners fit perfectly (**11–38**).

The top posed a new set of challenges. To meet these, I resorted to pattern felt. After making a 45-degree cut in the end of a piece of felt, I held it against the intended joint with the lacewood and folded the 45-degree cut over the edge and around the corner. Then I made a mark at the center of the curved edge (**11–39**). Using that mark, I cut the felt at right

11-37. Adding a "key stone" to permit the use of shorter veneers.

11-38. A closeup showing the fit of the chest border pieces.

angles with the edge that was held against the lacewood. Marking the veneer with the resultant pattern, I cut the first piece of border. After bonding this first piece next to the field, I wet it and rolled it over the edge and

11-41. A close-up of the fit of the corner.

11-39. Marking a pattern to be used to cut the corner pieces.

11-40. Checking the fit of the pattern on the opposite edge.

around the corner, being careful that each tiny area was bonded before preceding. Loose spots in the rounded edge would be all but impossible to correct.

The first time I tried bending veneer

lengthwise over a curved edge like this, I didn't wet it sufficiently. The face of the veneer fractured slightly, leaving tiny slivers standing. In the years that followed, I've used plenty of water and even let it soak in for a minute or two.

Next, I turned the pattern over and checked the fit. The fit was good except in the area marked with a chalked arrow in **11–40**. The first piece was a bit long in this area because I had to force the veneer around that double-curved spot. After cutting the second piece, I trimmed about 3/32 inch at the point of the arrow. Did the second cut fit? Take a look at **11–41**. Some of the pieces became slightly distorted as I bonded them. To check each to make sure a good joint would result, I used the straight edge of a piece of felt (**11–42**).

As I fit each of the corners first, I was left with four areas to fill in that were closed at both ends. To accurately cut the fill, I scribed the void onto felt (**11–43**). Then, using my straightedge held over the scribed line, I transferred the mark to the veneer (**11–44**).

No, all did not go perfectly. In instances where the fill was a bit long, I was able to compress it into place. In those other places, a sliver worked (**11–45**).

11-42. Using a piece of felt to check the joints.

11-44. Transferring the mark to the veneer.

11-43. Scribing the void onto a piece of felt.

11-45. A sliver is used to fill an open joint.

ADDING A FINISH

After a good sanding, I gave the chest a very weak but penetrating coat of bright-orange dye stain. This developed the iridescence of the veneer. It developed to such an extent that the effects were quite harsh; the contrast between the diamonds made them look like completely different woods. After sealing and sanding the chest, I gave it a coat of burnt-umber glazing stain. The glaze was brushed on and almost completely wiped off. The tiny bit that remained on the surface softened the diamonds considerably, and the stain left in the pores developed the grain pattern most beautifully.

CHAPTER 12

KIDNEY-SHAPED DESK

I f you have never worked with curved cabinetry, consider this project (**12–1 to 12–3**) for your first time out. It is not as difficult as one might think. Although the case is curved, the drawers are square and fit into square openings. The only challenge comes in fitting the drawer fronts, and that is not so difficult.

My client chose nara as the field veneer for the case. This was bordered with movingue in the front and zebrawood to the rear, around the drawers. Strips of mahogany were used to make the legs appear to flow into the case. I had olive ash burl and my client agreed to use that for the top.

12-1 to 12-3 (next page). Three views of the curved desk, which is made of 3/8-inch-luan "bender board." Shown here is a front view.

Knowing that this desk would receive tender loving care, I chose to bond the case veneers with contact cement. The nara and movingue veneers were very flat, so I anticipate no challenges. Besides, the speed of working with contact cement would make up for some of the other challenges that I mention below.

12-2. A closeup of the top of the desk.

12-3. A rear view of the desk.

PREPARING THE FORM
FOR THE CURVED CASE

Layout

My client furnished general specifications. The desk could be no more than 54 inches wide, about 28 inches deep, must have two file drawers for hanging files, two drawers for storage, and a pencil drawer in the center, and must have plenty of knee room.

The next morning, I placed a sheet of particleboard on a pair of sawhorses and went to work. First, I laid out a centerline and the width and length extremities I had to work with, along with a 24-inch kneehole. Then I began making light pencil lines, locating the drawers—making sure there would be plenty of room for files. Working on the curved outline of the case, my lines increased in darkness as I arrived at the final shape (**12–4**).

When I found satisfaction with the outline, I drove some small finishing nails at 3-inch intervals along the darkest line and stretched a piece of $5/8$-inch band steel along them. This would ensure that the desk would have a smooth curve. I then marked the outline of the band steel with a red pencil to keep from confusing the final shape with all of the preliminary lines (**12–5**).

Using a tape measure, I plotted several points on the right side of the center so that I could draw a line to cut along that would leave me plenty of room for waste.

Cutting the Form

Using my saber saw, I cut out the left half of the desk to about 1 inch beyond the centerline as accurately as possible and freed the piece from the sheet by cutting along the plotted line on the right. I also cut in about $1/8$ inch along

the centerline. This would ensure that I never lost the centerline and could find it from both sides of the piece. Then I smoothed any irregularities in the cut with a horseshoe rasp (**12–6**).

At this point, I had a piece of particleboard, half of which could be used as a template. This piece I screwed to the opposite corner of what was left of the sheet of particleboard using four $1 5/8$-inch drywall screws. Then with a $1/2$-inch straight cutter in my router, I followed the smoothed outline of the template, letting the bit's shank run on the template (**12–7**). As my bit had only about $3/8$ inch of cutting flutes, I had to make several passes at increasing depths.

I could have rough-cut with a saber saw and used a router and flush trimmer—the bearing riding on the template—but I have an aversion for saber saws and resort to them when there is no alternative.

With the cut made, I marked the centerline through the saw kerf I described above. After flipping the template over, I again screwed it to the other sheet and cut the opposite side. Now, I was able to turn the assembly over and cut the rest of the first piece using the second as a template.

While the pieces were screwed together, I did some more layout work, marking the exact location of the drawers, letting the lines flow to the extremes of the piece and then continuing them vertically on the edges of both pieces (**12–8**).

WORKING WITH THE FORM

Assembly

After cutting eight pieces of 2 x 4 to length, I passed one edge of these pieces over the jointer several times to cut back beyond the eased

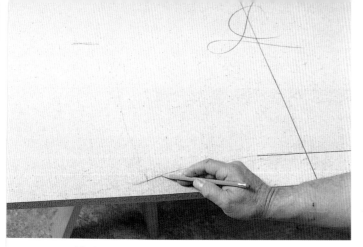

12-4. Drawing a pattern for the desk.

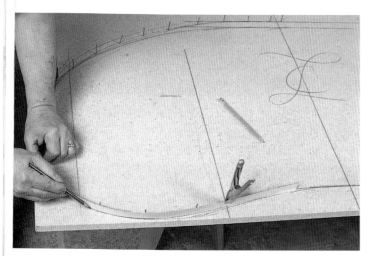

12-5. Marking an outline along the band steel.

12-6. Smoothing the cut with a rasp.

12-7. Cutting, using a template and a router.

12-8. The lines locating the position of the drawers have been marked.

12-36. Using a shooting block on the joint edge.

12-38. Flattening the bulge in the second veneer cut with a roller.

12-37. Setting the second veneer cut in position.

12-39. Using the back of a linoleum knife to smooth the veneer joint.

shooting block over the joint edge (**12–36**).

With the first cut down, I set the second in position. Illus. **12–37** shows the steel rod placed about an inch from the joint. After rolling down the bulk of the second cut, I withdrew the rod and used a roller on the bulge it left. With my free hand, I made sure that the second cut didn't ride up over the first (**12–38**).

To make certain that both edges of the joint were firmly bonded and the surfaces even, I made a firm pass down the joint with the back of a linoleum knife (**12–39**).

The third and fourth veneer cuts presented a little challenge, as there was a small, severely wrinkled patch on both. Normally, I would have discarded those pieces, but have included them here for demonstration purposes. First, I moistened the area. Then I quickly warmed it with an iron set on

12-40. Smoothing out a wrinkled spot.

12-41. Trimming the ends of the veneer cuts.

12-42. Finishing the bonding process with a piece of scrap.

one-quarter heat. Going to the edge of the wrinkled patch, I began to rock the iron back and forth lengthwise, slowing advancing it across the wrinkled path (12–40).

With all the pieces of the field in place, I then trimmed the ends. Illus. 12–41 shows pushpins being used to prevent the straight-edge from drifting. I had been using a veneer saw for cutting the joints, but noticed that I wasn't making much progress with it cutting across grain. To speed things, I switched to my "one-tooth-saw."

Removing the slip stick was a bit of a challenge, especially in the area that was ironed. But with a little twisting and tugging, it did come out.

In the previous photos you've seen me using a roller to bond the veneer cuts. That isn't quite enough pressure to do the job completely. Were I to apply sufficient pressure to the roller, the roller would break apart. Often, I use my veneer hammer to complete the job, but on this occasion it was covered with hide glue from a previous project. Rather than

clean it, I selected a soft pine scrap and proceeded to finish the job of bonding (12–42). How much pressure do you apply? Don't break the stick; just bend it a lot.

The thin strips of border went down quite easily. I first mitered one end of the border with the paper cutter. Then, using plenty of slip sticks, I started at the mitered end and set the piece in place, forcing it against the field

12-43. Setting a border piece in place.

12-45. Using the top of the linoleum knife to flatten the border veneer.

12-44. Using the back of a linoleum knife on the border veneer.

12-46. Making a miter cut on the end of a veneer border piece.

12-47. Trimming the borders.

12-48. Wiping the border surfaces with lacquer thinner removes the dust and reactivates the glue.

for a tight joint (**12–43**). Keeping a tight joint did cause some buckling of the strip, but as soon as the bonding pressure was applied, the buckles went down. Had they refused to go down, I would have again recruited the warm iron. It would relax the fibers of the veneer and make the contact cement more active.

Again, I used my linoleum knife to make sure the joint was well flattened. In this case, the veneers had such dramatic differences in thickness, I could only run the back of the knife on the border veneer (**12–44**). In a couple of spots, the joint was so tight that the back of the knife would not force that last little bit down. Here I used the top of the knife, rolling it over any high spots next to the joint (**12–45**).

With each piece of border, I cut the miter on only one end. After the piece was down, I cut the miter at the other end, using the lines I have extended onto the field as guides (**12–46**).

With all the borders down, I did the necessary trimming with my hook knife (**12–47**).

At this point, I had to leave the project overnight. The next morning, the contact cement was overly dry and some dust had settled on it. No problem. Rather than give all the pieces another coat of contact cement, I

12-49. Setting down the next field.

wiped the surfaces with a cloth dampened with lacquer thinner (**12–48**). This not only cleaned off the dust but reactivated the contact cement.

After setting the strip of mahogany above the leg and the movingue border piece next to it, I put down the next field in almost the same manner as the first (**12–49**). I did have to use some masking tape to prevent the slip sticks and rod from falling off the case.

After the case was complete, I started on

12-50. Using a hammer to bond zebrawood veneer to the drawer-front face edges. The hammer has a large, smooth surface that won't put a ding in the veneer.

12-53. Marking the MDF top using a pair of dividers.

12-51. Removing overhang on the drawer-front face.

12-52. Trimming the zebrawood border on the drawer fronts.

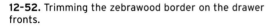

12-54. Trimming the pieces added to the top.

12-55. Trimming away a section of the veneer too extensively damaged the patch.

the drawers. Here, the first step was the facing of the edges of each drawer front with zebrawood. Working with a full cut of zebrawood, I encouraged it to stick with a hammer rather than a roller (**12–50**). As the veneer would be exposed to considerable stress in trimming, I wanted it bonded as completely as possible. The small hammer I'm shown using in **12–50** has a large, smooth surface that won't put a ding in the veneer. I've tried rubber hammers, but found that they can bend the veneer over the edge, causing it to fracture.

Next, I bonded and trimmed the facing and used a shooting block to remove any slight overhang (**12–51**). Then I placed the drawers in their compartments and worked them as if they were a single piece, much the same as I did the case. After the field was in place and trimmed as a unit, the last to go on was the zebrawood border. It too was worked and trimmed as if the drawer fronts were one piece (**12–52**).

WORKING WITH THE TOP

I set the case on top of a sheet of ³/₄-inch MDF. Using a pair of dividers set for the amount of overhang I wanted, I marked the MDF (**12–53**).

I really wanted a 1-inch top for the desk, so I "beefed up" the ³/₄-inch stock by adding pieces of ¹/₄-inch MDF around the edges. I let the pieces hang over slightly, and then trimmed them with a router and flush trimmer (**12–54**).

I next prepared the first two cuts of patched and flattened veneer by trimming away an area that was just too ugly to patch (**12–55**). This is one place where a clear straightedge comes in very handy, because it lets me see the whole veneer as I'm working.

12-56. Marking the location of the joint for the veneer cuts.

12-57. Spreading glue on the veneer.

Aligning the pieces for a good pattern match, I marked the location of the joint on the second cut. As shown in **12–56**, I also marked the face side boldly with chalk. You'll note that I accidentally spread glue on the face side over the chalk mark.

Now for the fun part: spreading the glue. Again, I let the veneer hang over the edge and brushed the glue toward that edge (**12–57**).

As I was spreading yellow glue for the dry-glue process, the moisture from the glue

12-58. Spraying the face side of the veneer with water to prevent it from curling.

12-59. Spreading glue on the field area of the border.

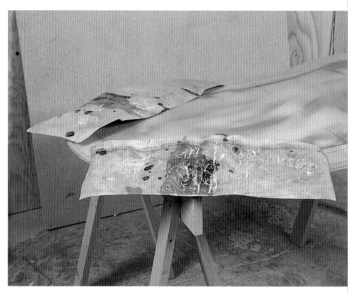

12-60. The two outer cuts of veneer became very wrinkled.

12-61. Using a hair drier to make the veneer cuts pliable.

began to penetrate the veneer, and the veneer began to curl; this condition was eased by spraying the face side with water (**12–58**). As the glue dried, I kept an eye on the veneer, and if the curling continued, I simply sprayed a little more water. Spraying that face side must be done carefully; try to avoid the tape. If the tape gets too wet, it will turn loose. Patches will fall out, and the veneer can look very ugly. Use only enough water, and take heart; the second coat of glue will not cause nearly as much curling. And be sure to let the first coat dry before applying the second; remember that "dry" means no opaque areas.

Before spreading glue on the top, I marked the border and spread glue only on the field area (**12–59**). I like the glue to be less than eight hours old when bonding, and I wasn't sure that I would get to the border for several days.

After the second coat of glue dried, I put all of the veneers between pieces of coated ³/₄-inch particleboard with a weight on top. The weight coupled with the residual moisture in the veneer helped flatten it substantially. In

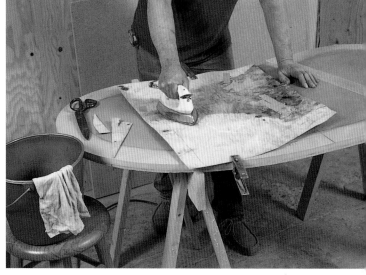

12-63. Bonding the veneer to the top using an iron.

the case of the two outer cuts, I was afraid that their severe wrinkling would cause breakage if placed under the particleboard (**12–60**).

A little heat from my industrial-strength hair dryer made these two veneer cuts pliable enough for the flattening operation (**12–61**). Pieces with dried glue can also be placed in the hot-plate press described in Chapter 6. Should you try this, be sure to put the glued side down, against a sheet of plastic film. The glue will stick well enough to the aluminum plate that removal can damage the veneer.

Before beginning the bonding, I ran a sanding block over the surface of the top (**12–62**). This was to cut the top off any particles that might have settled on the drying glue. If it were possible, I would have also passed the block over the veneer, but it was too wrinkled. To remove any dust produced by sanding, I wiped the surface with a damp cloth. That little bit of dampness also seemed to make the bonding go easier.

After positioning the first cut and securing it with a couple of spring clamps, I began ironing it down, working from the center outward (**12–63**).

I intentionally left this piece a little wrinkled just to show that a cut in this bad shape can be bonded successfully.

12-62. Using a sanding block to remove imbedded dust from the top's surface in preparation for veneer bonding.

12-64. To compress the areas that were still standing, it was necessary to lean on the iron while heating the veneer.

12-67. Replacing the joint's glue.

12-65. Putting down the bubbles remaining on the veneer.

12-68. Bonding the outer veneer cut to the top.

12-66. Trimming the veneer joint.

12-69. Completing the veneer joint.

12-70. Bonding the opposite veneer cuts.

The bonding did take effort. After I did all I could with the dry veneer, I trimmed the joint and wetted a portion of it that was about three times the size of the iron's base. As the water soaked in, the veneer began to expand and a couple of bubbles immediately appeared. I could also hear some clicking, indicating that other areas were pulling loose. Heating the whole area, I began to lean on the iron (**12–64**). The moisture and heat made the veneer much more pliable, and the pressure of the iron caused compression of the areas that were standing. The heat also caused the veneer to dry quickly, aiding in its natural tendency to hold its shape. I continued ironing until all of the clicking stopped.

As I ironed over the wet veneer, I removed the tape and wetted the area under the tape. With a little water and heat, the tape peeled off easily.

After working the entire panel, I detected a few persistent bubbles. These I wet. Then I heated the area and used extra pressure from the tip of the iron to put them down (**12–65**).

I had pre-trimmed this cut for the outer-veneer joint, but after ironing out all those wrinkles, the joint was no longer straight. It was a simple matter to trim an additional 1/16 inch from the joint. As shown in **12–66**, for this operation I used a linoleum knife and tilted the blade toward the straight edge for accuracy. I also pinned that slippery, plastic straightedge in place.

The waste from the joint came away, taking with it glue right down to the substrate. This is replaced by running a tiny bead of glue down the joint and smoothing it out with my finger (**12–67**).

I then proceeded with the outer veneer cut, bonding the area opposite the joint. Illus. **12–68** shows a steel rod under the veneer, about 1 1/2 inches from the joint. This was placed to make sure the veneer buckled and had a little extra length to make a compressed joint. The rod was probably a bit redundant, because there were plenty of wrinkles in the cut to provide compression.

Nonetheless, after the outer area was bonded, the rod was withdrawn and the joint was then completed (**12–69**). I then worked the veneer cuts on the opposite side of the joint in the same manner (**12–70**).

Once the field was down, I trimmed its outer edges for the border, using a needle scribe (**12–71**). For the most part, I was able to cut

12-71. Trimming the outer edges of the top, for the border.

12-77. The chalk marks indicate the grain pattern of the borders.

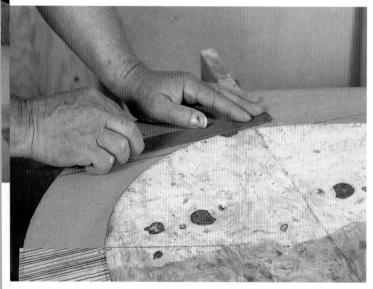

12-78. Touching up the field with a file.

12-79. Using an iron to ensure that the borders are bonded at the joint.

12-80. Checking for loose spots on the top.

To perhaps simplify things a bit in this border-fitting operation, it should be noted that the border pieces should fit well to the field. Minor putty patching can be done because the putty will not be obvious where the character of the veneer changes as dramatically as it did in this project.

To make the border more attractive, the grain pattern at the joints should form an isosceles triangle (**12–77**). This was my goal, but in several instances I fell short. I didn't go back to attempt corrections because, in a top this "busy," only the most critical examiner will note this inadequacy.

My trimming with the needle scribe generally worked well, although in a couple of places the cut needed touchup. In one area, a knot deflected the scribe, leaving a small area that was slightly long. This was easy to correct using the edge of a flat file (**12–78**). I could have used the folded edge of stiff sanding cloth or the edge of sandpaper folded over a block, but I find the file easier to handle.

Throughout the border installation, I found the zebrawood to be substantially thinner than the burl field. To ensure that the border was bonded at the joint, I held the iron on edge and ran it along the joint (**12–79**); and, to provide for compressed joints in the border, I began ironing from the side opposite the joint. As the slight wrinkles in the veneer were ironed out, the joint was compressed slightly.

After the top was complete, I checked for any loose spots by lightly passing the extended points of a pair of dividers lightly over every square inch of the top (**12–80**). A hollow sound under the dividers will quickly point out any loose spots. These I marked with chalk. Then I came back and wetted and ironed the areas.

ADDING A FINISH

After what seemed like days of sanding, I applied a thin coat of amber dye stain to the case and a thin coat of amber with a touch of brown to the top. The stain on the case brightened the movingue and accented the nara. Staining the top softened the contrast between the burl and zebrawood, which was quite stark.

After sealing and sanding, gloss lacquer was used to "build" the finish. The case was final-coated with a satin finish, and the top, after receiving many coats of gloss, was wet-sanded and then coated with a satin finish.

CHAPTER 13

ROUND DINING TABLE

Through the years, I've built many pedestal tables, but the design I'll describe here is one I rather enjoy. This is probably because I don't have to mount a 50-pound block of wood on the lathe to turn the pedestal. And I think that if I were offered a commission to build a solid-oak pedestal table, I'd turn it down. I've used so much oak in my lifetime that I now find it the most boring species I can think of—except when used for bending. For this table (**13–1 to 13–3**), I chose substrates of MDF, bender board, and

13-1 to 13-3 (following page). Three versions of the pedestal, or round dining table. The table itself is made of MDF, bender board and poplar. Zebrawood is used for the vertical surfaces, movingue for the base components and border, and Benin (tigerwood) for the sunburst. A bent piece of butternut is used to separate the movingue from the Benin sunburst.

13-2.

13-3.

poplar, and I used alder for the cove mold components; there was no particular reason for choosing the poplar and alder other than it's what I had on hand.

I chose zebrawood for the vertical surfaces and movingue for the base components. Benin

was my choice for the sunburst. I have used mahogany crotch for several sunburst tabletops, but the crotches—like oak—are becoming boring. Movingue was used for the border. I used a bent piece of butternut to separate the movingue from the Benin sunburst.

PREPARING THE PEDESTAL AND BASE

I always start this type of project with a full-scale drawing. To the left in **13–4** I have drawn the pedestal, and to the right one-quarter of the base. One critical component would be a piece of cove molding that I would cut on the table saw by passing the stock diagonally over the blade, lifting the blade in very small increments after each pass. I sketched this piece of cove using the saw blade I intended to use; this is also shown in **13–4**. This assured me that the molding could be cut, and also gave me an idea of what angle at which to set the saw guide.

13-4. Making a full-scale drawing for the dining table. A saw blade that will cut the cove molding is being used to check the curve.

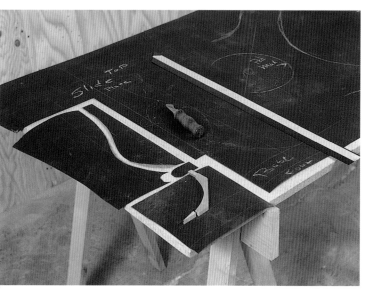

13-5. Shown on the left of the workbench is the cut pedestal pattern. On the right is the pattern for the base.

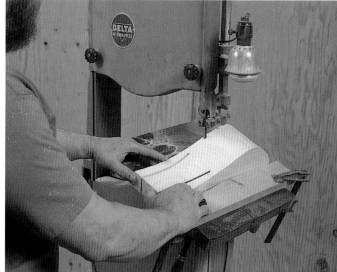

13-7. Finishing the angle cut using a band saw.

13-6. Marking the components of the pedestal.

13-8. Gluing the dado cut to receive the spline.

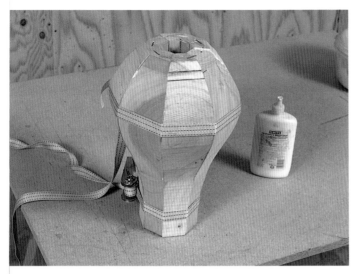

13-9. The assembled pedestal.

13-10. Cutting one-quarter of the base pattern.

13-11. Laying out the entire base.

I cut out the pedestal pattern and used the remaining sketch to check the fit of end cuts taken from the cove mold components (**13–5**). It should be noted that I checked several lumberyards for a piece of stock cove that would work. And after the slow process of cutting that cove on the table saw, I made a mental note to take the time to grind knives for any molding machine, should I ever have to do it again.

Pedestal

The next step was to mark the components of the octagonal pedestal, using the inside of the blank as a reference (**13–6**). These were glued up from two pieces of 8/4 poplar, one piece cut to exact length and the other long enough to accommodate the shape.

After cutting the blank using a band saw, I cut the 22 1/2-degree angle on a 10-inch table saw with the blade as high as it would go. The cut was then finished on a band saw (**13–7**).

Any irregularities from the band saw were removed with a block plane. Then the components were returned to the table saw and a dado cut made to receive a 1/4-inch spline. The spline does have some structural value and as such, it should be glued into the dado (**13–8**). It also helps to locate all of the pieces during assembly. I then spread a generous coat of glue on the side opposite the spline and on the spline groove, and assembled the pedestal (**13–9**).

Base

While the glue was drying on the pedestal, I cut out one-eighth of the base pattern. Then, scoring it at its center and folding it over, I used it as a pattern to complete the cutting of one-quarter of the pattern (**13–10**). I used this quarter section to lay out the complete base on a sheet of 3/4-inch MDF (**13–11**).

13-23. Putting the veneer cut down on the base.

13-25. Trimming a long spot in the veneer with a utility knife.

13-24. Rolling the veneer over the front edge.

Before trying to roll this cut over the foot end, I wet that section to make it more pliable. I then rolled the veneer over the edge, making sure that it was tightly bonded as I progressed (**13–24**).

In one small area the veneer was slightly long, a condition quickly rectified with a utility knife (**13–25**). Had it been slightly short, I would have left it and rolled the next cut into the void.

In the same manner, I proceeded to cut and bond all four of the longer cuts for the base. These could have been installed without the pattern. Oversized pieces could have been bonded and then trimmed, using a bent straightedge. However, the pieces in between them necessitated the pattern. Scribing these went far easier because there was the edge of the installed veneer for the divider point to ride along.

Illus. **13–26** shows the parallel lines near the center of the felt. These lines, made with the extended points of the dividers, are the first mark I make on any pattern. It tells me the setting of the dividers, should I suspect that they have drifted in handling or should I want to reset them for a longer or shorter cut.

13-26. Scribing the shorter veneer pieces.

13-28. Cutting out the top halves.

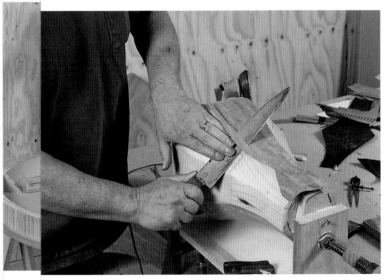

13-27. Trimming the oversized pieces for the pedestal.

BOMBE

T his project (**14–1** and **14–2**) was inspir[ed] by a fortunate lumber purchase. I w[as] able to pick up a quantity of partially a[ir] dried 3 x 6s at a price one-fifth that of any oth[er] lumber. Normally, I wouldn't think of buildi[ng] furniture with lumber that is not thorough[ly] cured, but I wanted to try an antique reprodu[c]tion and see if I could contend with the cha[l]lenges faced by woodworkers of old.

I also used twenty-five 1 x 8 x 8-foot piece[s] knowing that I would need some 1-inch mat[e]rial for drawer bottoms, backing, etc.

DRAWINGS AND PATTERNS

After a couple of lines and rough dimensio[ns] on a piece of paper, I proceeded to make a ful[l] scale drawing. Because I only like to draw onc[e] I made the drawing on a piece of 15-poun[d] roofing felt from which I could remove pa[t]terns for cutting the individual pieces of th[e] chest. You may be partial to drawing on larg[e] pieces of wrapping paper or cardboard, but giv[e] the felt a try. It is economical and far more su[b]

VENEERING THE PEDESTAL

After veneering the base, the pedestal was easy. Here, I bonded oversized pieces to every other section, trimming them after bonding. The unusual trimming instrument shown in **13–27** is a razor-sharp French chef's knife.

When held flat against the next section, it trims true and clean.

After bonding, trimming, and sanding the edges of the first four sections flush, I spread a tiny bead of glue over the bare edges of the newly bonded veneer, smearing it out with my finger. I then bonded the remainder, letting them overlap the edges of the first, and then continued trimming, sanding, etc.

BUILDING THE RIM

Even though there was still some work to do on the base, it was time to get the glue drying on some of the other components, mainly the rim. I cut out the halves of the top using a router (**13–28**), and on the underside of one of the halves I mounted some reusable MDF fixtures, constructing a form for the bent rim. Around these I bent and clamped three layers of 3/8-inch bender board, to form the table rim (**13–29**).

If I had an 8 x 4-foot piece of bender board on hand, I could have cut 6-foot

13-46. Using lacquer thinner on the base surface eliminate the dirt spots.

14-2. A closeup of the top of the chest.

13-47. The completed base with drilled dowels on t pedestal. Also shown is the bead character.

14-3. Flattening the felt.

14-4. Drawing an outline of the stock on the felt.

ASSEMBLING THE BASE

I'd been putting it off, but it was now tin finish the sanding on the base and assemb Movingue is one of those veneers that l blotchy where it is being sanded; there ap to be dark patches that could be dirt spot scorch marks from the iron. After doing thought was necessary with the sandpap wet the surface with lacquer thinner to s the spots would disappear (13–46).

stantial than paper for patterns. It does have the disadvantage of not being erasable, but that can be overcome with the use of different-colored pencils and scribing devices—as you will see.

After flattening the felt by pulling it over the sharp edge of the bench (14–3), I trimmed the left edge square with the bottom. I then drew in the chest top—30 inches from the bottom. Then, placing a piece of the actual stock I would be using on the felt, I outlined it in red

(14–4). (This piece of stock was cut from one of the more twisted 3 x 6s, faced on the jointer, and planed, giving me an idea of the maximum dimensions I would have to work with.) Normally, I would outline the stock with a scribing knife for a more accurate line, but I used the red pencil for benefit of the photos.

Next, within the confines of the marks of the stock, I drew a bold curved line and then marked out the approximate position of three graduated

14-5. Marking out the position of the drawers and skirt.

14-6. Modifying the line where the skirt meets the sides.

14-7. Marking the felt along the band steel with a linoleum knife.

drawers and the skirt (**14–5**). This would leave a leg approximately eight inches long that would flow into the skirt. It was then I noticed that there would be too little area where the skirt joined the sides. Not being able to erase my original line for the side curve, I modified it using a different-colored pencil (**14–6**).

If you are making a drawing like this, at any point you can stop, pin it to the wall, and stand back to get a truer perspective.

To make sure the curve was smooth, I drove a number of #3 finishing nails along it and bent a piece of ⅝-inch band steel along the nails. (You may notice in the photos that the band steel has been covered with a piece of masking tape. This was done to make the steel show against the black felt and also because in the following photos the steel will be used as a measuring device. Pencil marks will be made on the masking tape.) Two of the nails did not fall in

line with the steel. These were replaced by two that did. After all nails were in contact with the steel, I lightly marked the felt along the band steel with the point of a linoleum knife (**14–7**)—although a scribing knife or needle would work as well.

It was then a simple matter to pull the nails and cut the line. As the knife cut partially through the felt in the marking operation, it followed the partial cut accurately and effortlessly on the second pass.

Straight cuts were then made on the red lines marked on the stock, releasing a piece of felt that could be used as a pattern for the side and front of the leg. I fastened the waste felt that I'd cut from the left side of the pattern to the right of the pattern, using masking tape on its underside. This, incidentally, is what is going to happen with the wood. The waste will be glued back to the stock to complete the leg.

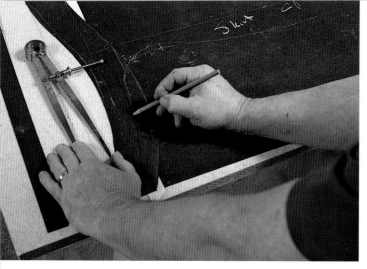

14-8. Drawing the inside part of the chest on the felt.

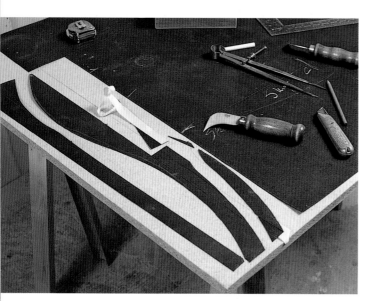

14-9. The cut patterns.

14-10. The rough-cut chest components set on stickers to acclimatize.

14-11. Drawing a leg pattern on the stock face.

14-12. Marking the leg blank using a pair of dividers.

14-13. Another way of marking the blank is to mark its middle and use the leg pattern to mark the rest of it.

After positioning the leg pattern back onto the drawing, I used a pair of dividers to scribe a line parallel to the side of the leg. (Although the leg will be tapered, it's easier to draw that taper with the parallel line as a reference.) Again using a colored pencil, I finished drawing the inside of the leg flowing into the skirt (14–8).

After I finished cutting the patterns (14–9), I had a good idea of the rough sizes of the material that would be needed. I left the patterns/drawings and went to the lumber pile, where I cut the rough lengths and placed sticks between them to let the pieces acclimatize somewhat (14–10). The thickness of the 1 x 3 would remain wet longer than the width.

PREPARING THE COMPONENTS

Side Pieces

Once the stock was faced and planed to provide clean, parallel surfaces with square corners, the first step was to mark out the face of the side's core pieces. I used a square to draw a square line for the top edge and the upper part of the leg

pattern on the face of the stock (14–11). After the piece was cut, the resulting waste was glued to the back side of the blank, producing a piece of stock from which I could cut two side core pieces.

Illus. 14–16 shows the side pieces assembled with clamps.

Once out of the clamps, this blank was marked. (If you are a little careless and the pieces do not fit perfectly, it's a good idea to run the blank over the jointer to true the edge. Otherwise, the blank will teeter on the saw table and the cut won't be perpendicular with the edge.) There are two ways to do this. The first way consists of using a pair of dividers, one leg riding the face and the other making the mark (14–12). It is necessary that the dividers be kept perpendicular to the straight line of the joint, because keeping them perpendicular to the tangent of the curve will produce a curve different from the pattern.

Another way is to mark the center of the blank at several places and again use the upper part of the leg pattern to mark the rest of the blank (14–13).

In any event, make sure that the top of the

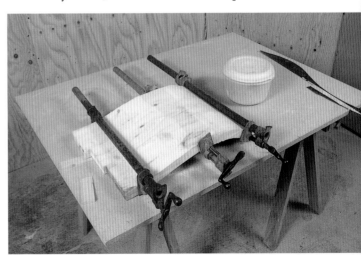

14-14. The assembled pieces for the side core.

pattern is placed accurately on the blank, as this top line will become the reference for all of the side components.

Once all the blanks were cut on the band saw, they were glued to form the core of the side (**14–14**). This was done very carefully, as I made sure that the top and face lined up as well as possible. Inconsistencies in thickness of the pieces I let show on the inside—I'd take care of that later.

Legs

I pinned the pattern to a piece of leg stock with the straight part of the pattern aligned with the back of the stock, and then marked only the face (**14–15**). After the cut was made, the lower piece of waste was glued back to the blank (**14–16**), providing a strengthening area for the lower inside of the leg.

Note the stick spanning the featheredge of the waste pieces. If you look carefully, you will also see some small nails driven partway through the waste. These are there to prevent the pieces from slipping in the glue as the clamps are applied. Another technique to keep the components from slipping is to rub the glued surfaces together, pull them apart, and let the glue "tack up" for a minute or so. In any event, apply the clamp pressure slowly, letting the excess squeeze out.

While the glue was drying on the legs, I took a few minutes to clean up the inside of the side core pieces. My inshave served well for the task (**14–17**), for the object was not to provide a perfectly smooth surface. Rather, I wanted to disguise the joints somewhat and remove any evidence of the yellow glue.

Once the glue was dry, I returned the pattern to the blank and marked out the full leg (**14–18**).

Now I chose to cut only two 5 1/2-inch-wide blanks. Ripping off the width required for a front leg left enough material for a back. This I did on the table saw—not the safest of operations. If you feel the least hesitant, either cut the legs individually or set up a rip fence on your band saw to accomplish the feat.

Finalizing the Case Sides

With the legs cut, I measured their combined width and cut the core blank to the proper width. All pieces prepared, I glued the components of the case side together (**14–19**). Care should be taken that they all are flush along the top. Otherwise, there will be work with a hand plane to true the top edge. You could, of course, pass the top of the side over the jointer, but I don't recommend it unless you are skilled and comfortable with such operations.

Caution: Be sure that you glue the sides up so that there is a pair consisting of one from each side rather than two of the same side.

Once the glue was dry, I marked out the cut needed at the front. Because the pattern was too short to conform to the curved surface that existed, I started the marking by setting the pattern flush with the bottom of the leg—straight portion against the joint between the leg and the core. After drawing the line about a third of the way up, I shifted the pattern so that the bulge lined up with the bulge of the case, continuing the line to the bulge (**14–20**). The final marking was done with the pattern flush with the top of the case.

Gluing Back the Waste

Once the front was cut, the waste had to be glued back to give enough stock to finish cutting the shape of the front leg—the front leg also needs a little extra strength at this point. This is a little tricky in that the waste piece will need to be notched out to fit around the core.

14-15. Marking the pattern on the face of the leg stock.

14-16. Spreading the glue for adding the waste.

14-17. Cleaning up the inside of the side core pieces with an inshave.

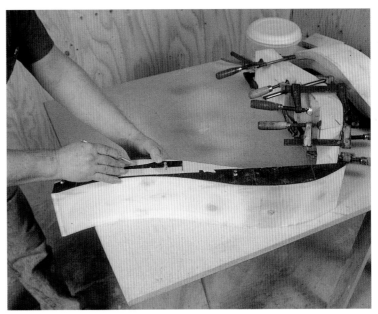

14-18. Marking out the entire leg.

14-19. The side components glued and clamped together.

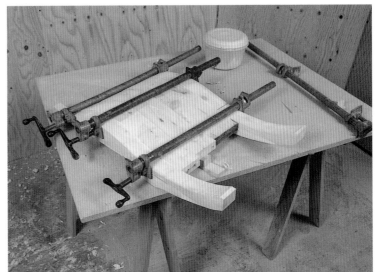

14-20. Drawing the pattern for the front.

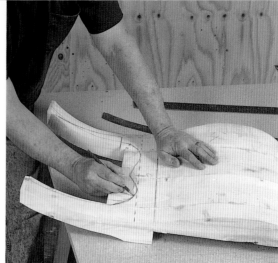

14-22. Sketching the scallop.

14-21. Marking the notch for the waste piece.

14-23. Marking the opposite side with a waste piece.

To mark the notch, I placed the waste above the position into which it must fall, set a pair of dividers to the amount of offset, and then scribed a line on the waste (**14–21**).

Cutting the Side Scallop

With the waste glued back, I sketched the scallop I wanted, marking my final decision with a red pencil (**14–22**). Saving the waste piece from the cut on the left side, I used it to mark the right (**14–23**).

After the scallop was cut, I got excited and spent a couple of minutes cleaning up the joints in the core and the legs with a hand plane (**14–24**).

Preparing the Lower Scalloped Rail

I returned to the felt and drew a pattern for the lower rail—which was also to be used for the upper rail. Knowing that I wanted a minimum drawer front thickness of 1 inch and that I had 2½-inch material to work with, I drew a curve

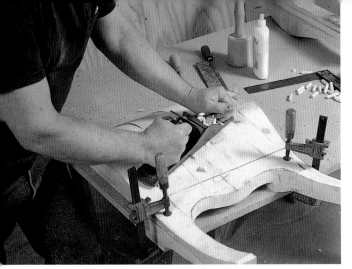

14-24. Cleaning up the joints in the legs and side pieces using a hand plane.

14-26. Marking a full piece of stock.

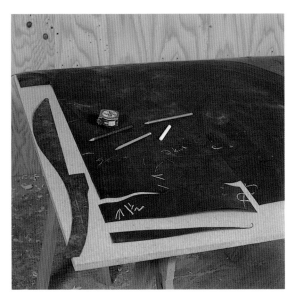

14-25. Drawing a curve for the lower scalloped rail.

14-27. Dowels have been marked in the end of the rail, and the side of the case has been marked with dowel points for boring.

that started 1½ inches back from the face, flowing to a bulge in the center (**14–25**). With the pattern I marked a full piece of stock (**14–26**), later ripping off a piece to be used as the back, lower rail. After cutting the face on a band saw, I sketched in the scallop and used the waste from one side to mark the other.

Next, I drilled holes for dowels in the end of the rail and, using dowel points, marked the side of the case for boring (**14–27**). To properly locate the piece, I held it parallel with the joint between the front leg and the core.

Preparing the Upper Rails

After drawing the location and angles of the drawer fronts and rails on the left leg, I assembled the pieces I had—without glue—to get an accurate measurement for the balance of the

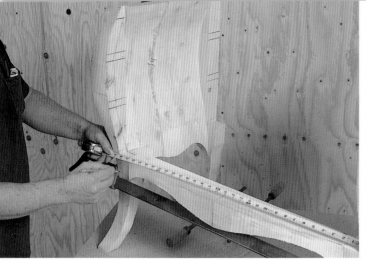

14-28. The components have been assembled so that the rails can be measured.

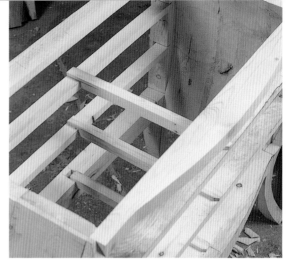

14-31. This view of the assembly shows how the rear rail floats in a mortise in the back legs.

14-29. Mate the tabs on the front legs with the back of each leg.

14-32. Rough drawer fronts fit to the case.

14-30. The assembled case.

14-33. Using a hand plane to dress up the drawer bottom.

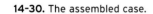

14-34. Beveling the drawer edge.

14-35. Shaping the drawer fronts using an air chisel and gouge.

rails (**14–28**). The front rails were also doweled into the case, but I also left a tab on the end of each that would be glued to the back of the leg (**14–29**).

ASSEMBLY

With glue and plenty of clamps, I assembled the case, making sure that the drawer openings were square (**14–30**). Illus. **14–31** shows how the upper rails are glued to the core. Also note that the rear rails float in mortises cut in the back legs. This will permit expansion and contraction of the sides without disturbing rails and drawer guides, which, at this time, are just set in place.

DRAWERS

With the case assembled, the next step was to fit the drawer fronts, using the red lines drawn in **14–28** to determine their size and angles (**14–32**). I was then able to cut the remainder of the drawer components with all required dadoes.

After cutting the dado in the drawer bottom, I decided to dress it up with a few marks from a hand plane (**14–33**), and then set about beveling the edge using a drawknife (**14–34**).

I assembled the drawers with nails that I set with an old screwdriver ground to resemble the head of a square hand-cut nail. When the nail holes are patched, they do appear to contain an old nail.

SHAPING THE DRAWER FRONTS

With the drawers in place, the next step was to shape the drawer front. This can be done with a mallet and gouge—if you're a purist and need the exercise. I prefer an air chisel with a gouge. Illus. **14–35** shows the wedges standing in the margins at the ends of the drawer fronts. These are in place to prevent the drawer from shifting in the opening and knocking the drawer guide out of alignment.

If the air chisel isn't enough to shape the drawer fronts, consider the angle grinder

14-42. A closeup of the drawer front shows a piece of veneer has been folded over.

14-45. Trimming off the ends of the veneer on the drawer fronts.

14-43. A closeup of the drawer front showing the folded area after sanding.

14-46. Bonding the end veneer to the case.

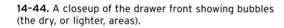

14-44. A closeup of the drawer front showing bubbles (the dry, or lighter, areas).

14-47. Cutting the ends of the drawer front so they will fit the borders.

I was more cautious with the other side of the drawer, spreading out potential creases and bubbles and making sure they were small enough to deal with. I allowed the tops of a couple of these bubbles to dry for demonstration purposes (**14–44**). Once these spots—which stood almost 3/16 inch high—were bonded, there was evidence of the compression, but it is very difficult to notice.

Once the veneer was completely bonded, I carefully trimmed off the ends with a veneer saw (**14–45**), marking each piece because I was not through with this cut of veneer. I installed the drawers and bonded each trimming to the case front adjacent to the drawer from where it came (**14–46**). The straight line at the juncture of the drawer ends and the case can be rather attractive in this type of construction, but continuing the veneer pattern of the drawer fronts to the border distracts the eye from the straight line.

Once all of the pieces were in place, I cut the ends with a scribe to fit the border (**14–47**). I did bond the pieces in several areas too strongly and had to use a chisel to free the areas that didn't separate easily (**14–48**).

As a precaution, I ran a veneer saw—one with set teeth—down the juncture of the drawer fronts and case, trimming off any overhang of the pieces just bonded (**14–49**). This was to prevent chipping of the newly bonded veneer when I removed the drawers.

Moving right along, I attacked the sides. After straightening the edges of the three pieces of veneer I intended to use, I bonded the center cut. I next bonded the second cut for about an inch along the joint, pulling the joint tight as I went (**14–50**). After the area along the joint was completely bonded, I went back and bonded the rest of the cut, forcing any wrinkles toward the joint. As there was no way to use a metal rod under the veneer to buckle it for a compressed joint, this technique was my second choice.

To trim the field for the border, I used a lit-

14-48. Freeing the ends with a chisel so they can be trimmed.

14-49. Trimming off the veneer overhanging where the drawer fronts and case meet.

14-50. Veneering the sides.

14-51. A closeup showing an errant scribing mark made when trimming the field for a border.

14-54. Pre-forming the veneer so that it will fit on the curve on the inside of the leg.

14-52. Using a wood-carving tool to smooth a curve.

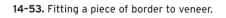

14-53. Fitting a piece of border to veneer.

14-55. The tools and items needed to veneer the top. They include a glue pot; a couple of plastic cups of glue flakes; an iron, shown bathing in about 1/4 inch of water contained in an old electric skillet; a new, nondisposable bristle brush; a shop-built veneer hammer; a automobile window scraper; a squeegee; a bucket filled with warm water; and a towel.

14-56. Dragging the teeth of the saw across the surface to "tooth" it.

tle scribe/cutter described in Chapter 2. Although it's a fine tool, it can be a bit challenging when used on tight curves. There is no way that it can cut too deeply, but it's possible it can start to follow the grain or, if not held at quite the right angle, not cut deeply enough (**14–51**).

In one area I was in such poor form that I had to smooth out the cut using a wood-carving tools (**14–52**).

Using a pair of dividers, I began scribing and fitting the pieces of border. As shown in **14–53**, many narrow pieces are used on the tight curves. This is necessary to make the border look it follows the curve. When finished, it will look even better from a distance than in the close-up photo.

Pressing the veneer into the tight curve on the inside of the legs posed another challenge because the iron could not heat enough of the surface quickly enough to make the veneer sufficiently pliable to conform to the sharp curve at the top. Here I did some pre-forming by heating the veneer on a flat surface, and then quickly bending it and clamping it into position (**14–54**). After it cooled, it fit the tight curve very nicely.

VENEERING THE TOP

It was finally time to veneer the top and get my hands covered with hide glue. Early in the morning, I set up a small table with the things I would need. Among the tools and items shown in **14–55** is a glue pot in the process of melting a fresh charge of rehydrated glue. Beside it, I put a couple of plastic cups of glue flakes. The cup to the left contains dry flakes, a few of which I scattered on the bench in front of it. The cup on the right contains flakes that soaked in water overnight. Both cups contained the same volume of flakes, so you can get an idea of the increased volume the soaking process produces.

Also shown is my iron, bathing in about 1/4 inch of water contained in an old electric skillet. The skillet is not heated; it just happens to be the only container I have that is big enough for the iron. The water bath will dissolve any hide glue that may accumulate and dry on the iron.

I also used a new nondisposable bristle brush. At the end of the session, I may wash it in warm water, or I may squeeze out all excess glue and let it dry. It will, of course, dry hard and appear to be ruined, but a couple of hour's soaking in cold water and gentle heating in hot glue will completely restore it.

Next to my shop-built veneer hammer is an automobile window scraper and squeegee. Just in case the veneer is very fragile, I'll use the scraper instead of the hammer.

Most important of all are the bucket filled with warm water and the towel. Should I get glue on my hands, I'll seek the refuge of the warm water to remove it—lest I'll not be able to let go of anything I may touch.

Before I started assembling the equipment, I gave the face side of the top a good coat of water to begin the pre-cupping. As I waited for the glue to melt, I kept wetting the top. After about an hour, the center was standing about 1/2 inch above the rest of the board; it was time to begin veneering.

Before beginning, I "toothed" the surface; that is, I cut some grooves to hold the glue. I've never had a toothing plane, but I find that dragging the teeth of a saw across the surface works very well (**14–56**). On another occasion, I may have, at this point, heated the top, but on this day the shop was a heavenly 85 degrees.

This particular top was somewhat challenging because I glued it up from boards that weren't completely dry. The knots were standing slightly proud, and two of the boards had cupped slightly—just what I hoped for.

Next, I sprayed the face side of the veneer and quickly spread glue on the top (**14–57**). If

14-57. Spreading glue on the top.

14-60. Trimming the veneer joint.

14-58. Smoothing out the veneer with the hands.

14-61. Using a hammer to ensure that the veneer joint fits properly.

14-59. Forcing out excess using a veneer hammer.

14-62. Using a clamp and a block of wood to press down one spot on the veneer.

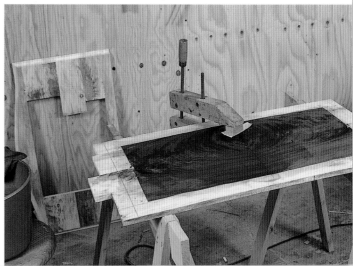

the face side is not wet, as the hot glue comes in contact with the back the veneer will curl, making it impossible to get down.

After the veneer was set in the hot glue, I passed my hands over it to push any large air bubbles and slide the cut into exact position (**14–58**). Then, starting at the center, I went to work with the hammer, squeezing excess glue to the edges of the cut and forcing the veneer down (**14–59**). I pulled the hammer both with the grain and across it, taking care to squeeze any thick spots of glue from around knots or in the bottoms of the cups. I picked up puddles of glue around the edges with a putty knife and return them to the pot.

At this point, I let the piece set for 15 minutes. Then I trimmed the joint at the centerline (**14–60**). I had let that first cut hang about ¼ inch over the centerline, and when I had first placed the cut, the edge was reasonably straight. After the 15 minutes of expansion, it was at least ³⁄₃₂ inch out of alignment.

Before trimming the joint, I had sprayed the face of the second cut and set it aside to expand a bit. After about five minutes, I trimmed it straight, spread glue on the substrate, and set the veneer in place. On the second cut, I began by working the area next to the joint, pulling with the hammer to make sure that the joint fit tightly (**14–61**). This is a little tricky in that the glue can only exit at the joint and can cause the veneers to overlap, but with a little care I've found it the best way to ensure a good, tight joint. After working the cut down, there was one tiny spot that refused to stick. For this, I enlisted the aid of a small block of wood and a clamp. Illus. **14–62** shows the piece of paper beneath the block to prevent it from sticking to the veneer.

It is fair to use a clamp or two in a hammer operation. Sandbags can also be used, and I have a couple of heavy babbit (a soft metal used for pouring bearings) ingots that I often press into service.

You may have noticed in the photographs that the substrate is not yet trimmed to size. The excess provides a place for the glue to go, rather than dripping onto the floor, or, more importantly, my shoes.

Nonetheless, I did have to cut the front edge to final shape so that I could use my cutter/scribe to prepare the field for the border. As shown in **14–63**, I have put a piece of veneer tape down the joint. I never rush to tape joints, because I want to make sure they aren't going to curl up before placing the tape. And just to make sure that the tape doesn't pull moisture from the joint, causing it to curl, I dip the tape in water rather than just moistening it. This also expands the tape and—hopefully—as it shrinks, it will pull the joint even tighter.

I cut the straight pieces of border with a paper cutter, but scribed the curved front pieces and cut them with scissors (**14–64**).

I put the border down working from the corners (**14–65**). This was to give each piece a chance to settle before placing one next to it. By the time I got to the border, there were quite a few bumps of glue in the border area that were dry. That's why the scraper was close at hand.

You'll also see in the photographs that I've moved that glue pot closer to hand, insulating it from the field with a block of wood. I always keep a stirring stick in the pot to stir in any scum that may form on the glue. But its most important duty is to prevent the brush from sliding to the bottom of the pot.

After securing clamps and blocks over a couple of joints that were starting to buckle, I trimmed the front edge using a utility knife (**14–66**). I prefer to use a downward slicing action rather than pulling the knife along the veneer. The warm, wet veneer slices easily, but

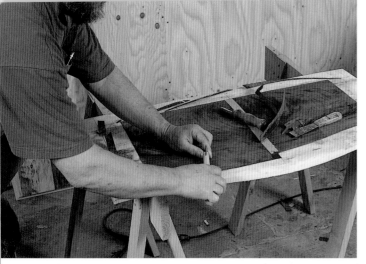

14-63. Trimming the field for the border.

14-66. Trimming with a utility knife.

14-64. Scribing a piece of veneer to the field.

14-67. Warming a loose spot in the field to put it down.

14-65. Hammering down a piece of border. Notice that the glue pot has been moved closer to hand, and is insulating from the field with a block of wood. Always keep a stirring stick in the pot to stir in any scum that may form on the glue and to prevent the brush from sliding to the bottom of the pot.

14-68. The boards fit into the bottom of the case serve as a dust protector.

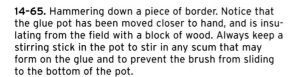

14-69. The backing is being installed.

14-70. Two x fours have been clamped to the top to prevent it from distorting.

will buckle if sideways pressure is applied to it.

As I was taping the border joints, I noticed a couple of loose spots in the field. Gently warming one with the iron, I held it down with my fingertips as I warmed the other (**14–67**). By this time, the glue under the veneer was drying so it was very viscous and sticky. With just that little amount of heat, it reactivated, and after a minute's worth of finger pressure, the veneer stayed down.

MAKING THE BACKING AND DUST PROTECTOR

As the top stood in the corner drying, I fit some ³/₈-inch tongue-and-groove boards into the bottom to form a dust protector and secured them with blocks dipped in hot hide glue (**14–68**).

After fastening the false top with a few small nails, I turned the case over and secured it with glue blocks, much the same as the dust protector. Then I installed the backing, which was also composed of ³/₈-inch tongue-and-groove boards (**14–69**). I fastened these with a pneumatic nailer, but then went back and set the nails with a screwdriver ground to look like the head of a square-cut nail.

Just before leaving the shop for the evening, I clamped the top between some 2 x 4s (**14–70**). Just in case my calculations were

wrong, I didn't want to return in the morning and find the top warped. I also put a piece of paper under the 2 x 4s to prevent them from sticking to any glue that might still be active.

After the top dried for several days, it would be only a matter of trimming it to size, running a router around it to cut a bead, and then fastening it to the false top with several slot-head screws. I must add that after I removed the 2 x 4s, the top did cup slightly, but the screws easily pulled it down.

ADDING A FINISH

Next came the sanding, and believe me, there was a lot of sanding. Not wanting to destroy the effect of the slightly high-standing knots—or cut through at those points—all sanding was by hand with a piece of soft sandpaper.

For a little accent and to soften the contrast, I gave the chest a wet coat of weak, light golden oak dye stain, followed by several coats of sanding sealer. All of the interior and drawers were generously sealed. For the purpose of **14–1** and **14–2**, I finished up with a coat of satin lacquer. (The light reflections off a high-gloss finish are just too much to contend with.) Eventually, I'll French-polish the piece. That will add authenticity, and I could use another workout.

INDEX

Abrasive devices, 42
Adhesives for bonding veneer and
    substrate
    properties of, 73, 74–75, 76
    types of, 76, 77–83, 84
Alder, 201
Antique tables, telegraphing in, 62
Apple/maple plywood, 63
Baltic birch plywood, 63
"Barking" logs, 15
Bender board
    as substrate, 63, 64
    using on desk, 174, 178, 179, 182
    using on dining table, 200
Benin, 200, 201
"Bird's mouth," 129
Blanket chest, veneering a
    assembly of, 167, 168–172, 173
    finish for, 173
    materials used for, 158, 159
    veneer layout and taping, 159,
        160–162, 163
    veneer, pressing, 163, 164–166,
        167
Bleach, lightening veneer with, 124
Bombé chest, veneering a
    assembly, 226, 227
    backing and dust protector,
        making the, 237
    components, preparing, 221,
        222–226, 227
    drawer fronts, shaping, 227, 228,
        229
    drawer fronts, veneering, 229,
        230–232, 233
    drawers, 226, 227
    drawings and patterns for, 217,
        218–219, 220
    finish, adding a, 237
    materials used for, 217
    top, veneering, 233, 234–236, 237
Book and butt match
    definition of, 13
    presentation, 9, 20
Book-matching
    cuts with slicing defects, 23, 24
    definition of, 13
    presentation of, 18, 19
Borders, tools used for making, 32,
    33
Brazilian rosewood, mineral
    deposits in, 22
Burls
    with book and butt match, 19, 20

definition of, 13, 33
    look at, 16
Butt, 13, 16
Butternut, 200
Carpathian elm, and holes, 223
Carving tools, 32, 33
Cauling, 98, 99, 153, 154
Checkerboard, veneering, 144,
    145–150, 151
Cherry, and sun fade, 22
Chipboard, 61
Circle devices, 40, 41
Circles, laying out on substrate,
    65, 66
Clamps, 42
Coasters, veneering, 140, 141–143,
    144
Color retention in veneer, 22
Combination stains, 123, 124
Compasses, laying out with, 65,
    66
Composites, shaping, 71
Compressed joints, 94
Contact cement
    bonding with, 83, 84, 95, 96
    characteristics of, 82, 83
    cleaning up, 84
    using on checkerboard, 146,
        147, 148, 149
Creep, 76
Cross-banded veneers, characteris-
    tics of, 24
"Crossbanding," 62
Crotch, 13, 16
Curves, laying out on substrate,
    66, 67
Cutting tools
    knives with disposable blades,
        27, 28
    linoleum knives, 28
    paper cutters, 32
    rotary cutters, 31
    scissors and snips, 32
    straightedges, 25, 26
    veneer saws, 29, 30, 31
Danish oils, 126
Desk, veneering a
    curved case, preparing the form
        for, 176, 177
    curved case, working with the,
        176, 177–190, 191
    materials for, 174, 175
Dining table, veneering a
    base, assembling the, 216

base, veneering the, 207, 208, 209
    finish, adding a, 216
    materials used for, 200, 201
    pedestal and base, preparing the,
        201, 202–206, 207
    pedestal, veneering the, 209
    rim, building the, 209, 210, 211
    top, laying out the, 211212, 213
    top, veneering the, 213, 214–215
Dividers, 39, 40, 41
Dry-glue bonding
    description of, 91, 92
    joints, 94, 95
    preparing the glue, 92, 93
    techniques, 93, 94
Drying time, 75
Drywall, as substrate, 65
Dye stains, 122, 123
Dyeing veneer, 52
Edge scribes, 40
End checks, 20, 21
Field, definition of, 13
Fillers, 125
Finish, adding a,
    to blanket chest, 173
    bleach, 124
    to bombé chest, 237
    to checkerboard, 149
    to coasters, 144
    to dining table, 216
    fillers, 124
    to lamp, 157
    oil finishes, 125, 126
    patching, 120, 121
    sanding, 121, 122
    to simple box, 140
    stains, 122, 123, 124
    topcoats, 126
Fir plywood, cross-banding, 62
Flake, 61
Flattening veneer, 44, 45–48, 49
Fretsaw, 128
Glass, as substrate, 65
Glazing stains, 124
Glue blocks, 74
Glue pot
    preparing hide glue in a, 78, 79
    using to bond, 89, 90
    using to veneer bombé chest,
        232, 233, 235, 236
Glue spreaders, 37, 38
Gouges, 33
Ground. See Substrates
Hammers, 41

Hardness of glue, 74
Hardware for veneered panels, 71
Hide glue, hot
    bonding techniques with, 84,
        85–89, 90
    characteristics of, 76, 77, 78
    cleaning up, 78
    experimenting with, 79, 80
    importance of, 76
    preparing, 78, 79
    and "sizing," 51
    and stainless-steel veneer saw, 30
    strength of, 77
    veneering molding with, 117
Hot pipe, 52, 53
Inlays
    techniques for making, 135, 136
    tools used to make, 32, 33
Inshave, 222, 223
Iron, household
    bonding borders with, 199
    bonding hide glue with, 86
    drying veneer tape with, 57
    setting tape on waste pieces
        with, 161
    using to fix border over round-
        ed edge, 169
Jeweler's saw, 128, 129
"Key stone," 171
Koa, mineral deposits in, 22
Lacewood
    used for blanket chest, 158, 159
    thin spots in, 21
Lacquer as topcoat, 126
Lamp, veneering a, 150–157
    base, cutting veneer for the, 157
    blank, cutting, 151, 152, 153
    final procedures, 154, 155
    pattern, 150, 151
    substrate preparation, 150, 151
    veneering, preparing the, 153, 154
Layout tools, 39, 40, 41
Linoleum knife
    marking felt with, 219
    smoothing a veneer joint with a,
        188, 188, 189
    tearing tape with, 160, 161
    trimming border veneer with,
        188, 189
    use in veneering, 28
Linseed oil, 126
Lumber-core plywood, as sub-
    strate, 63
Mahogany
    and sun fade, 22
    using on desk, 174
Man-made boards, as substrate, 62,
    63–64, 65

Maple, cross-banding with, 62
Marquetry
    adjusting curves, 131
    cutting curves, 128, 129–130
    inlay techniques, 135
    multi-cutting, 132, 133
    pad-cutting, 133, 134
    pattern-cutting, 131, 132
    reinforcing the pieces, 127, 128
    shading, 136
    window-cutting, 131, 132
Mechanical presses
    bonding using, 96, 97, 98
    using, 104, 105–106, 107
Medium-density fiberboard
    as substrate, 64
    using to make a mechanical
        press, 104
Metal, as substrate, 65
Mineral deposits in veneer, 22
Molder, 68
Moldings, 117, 118
Movingue veneer
    fine-tuning with a sanding
        block, 207
    using on dining table, 200, 201
Multi-cutting (marquetry), 132, 133
Nara
    and sun fade, 22
    using on desk, 174, 183
Oak, and sun fade, 22
Oil finishes, 125, 126
Olive ash
    and holes, 22, 23
    using on desk, 174
Open assembly time, 75
Ovals, laying out, 66
"Oyster shell," 13, 15
Pad-cutting (marquetry), 133, 134
Paper-backed veneers, 17, 24
Paper cutters, 32, 156, 157
Particleboard
    as substrate, 64
    as substrate, and edge treat-
        ments, 67, 68–69, 70
    used for veneer press, 97
Pattern-cutting (marquetry), 131
Pigmented stains, 122
Pine box, 138
Plain-sliced veneer, 12, 14, 15
Poplar
    and sun fade, 22
    using on dining table, 200, 201
Power sanding, 122
Pre-forming veneer, 52, 53
Press, mechanical
    bonding with, 96, 97, 98
    making a, 104–113

Pull, 59, 60
Punches, 33, 34, 35, 36
PVA glues
    characteristics of, 80
    cleaning up, 80
    dry-bonding with, 91, 92, 93, 94
Quartered figure, definition of, 13
Quarter oak, thin spots in, 21
Red oak, and sun fade, 22
Reversibility of glue, 76
Rift, definition of, 13
Rosewoods, oils and resins in, 20
Rotary-cut plywood, 61
Rotary cutters, 31
Rotary-sliced veneer, 13, 14, 15
Router
    cutting grooves in substrates
        with, 69
    cutting desk legs with, 180, 181
    cutting drawer dadoes with, 182,
        183
    cutting tubing groove with, 108
    trimming outer edges of dia-
        monds with, 166, 167
    trimming form with, 176, 177
Safety considerations, 10
Sanding, 120, 121
Sanding block
    making minor corrections with,
        197
    removing dust with, 193
Satinwood, 14, 20
Scissors and snips, 32
Scribing dividers, 39, 40
Scroll-saw, cutting veneer with,
    129, 130
Setting time, 75
Shading, 136
Shellac, as topcoat, 126
"Shooting" veneer, 54, 55
Simple box, veneering a, 138,
    139–140, 141
"Single-side," 48
"Sizing," 60
Slip match, 13, 18, 19
Solar press heat, 107, 108
Solid wood as substrate, 61, 62
Spiral veneering, 119
Splits in veneer, 20, 21
Stains, 122, 123, 124
Steam-"fired" heater, 108, 109–113
Steam generator, 114–116, 117
Straightedges, 25, 26, 27
Strengthening veneer, 50, 51–52, 53
Stump, look at, 16
Substrates
    to avoid, 60
    definition of, 59

drywall, 65
edge treatments, 67, 68–71, 72
glass, 64
layout technique, 65, 66, 67
man-made boards, 62, 63, 64
metal, 65
pull, 59, 60, 61
telegraphing, 61, 62
trimming and repairing, 72
Surface compression in veneer, 23
Tabletop diamond design, 19
Tape, veneer
reinforcing marquetry pieces
with, 127, 128
strengthening veneer with, 50, 51
Teak, 20
"Telegraphing," 61, 62
Tools and equipment
abrasive devices, 41, 42
carving tools, 32, 33
circle devices, 40, 41
clamps, 42
cutting surface, 32
edge scribes, 40
glue containers with spreaders, 37
hammers, 41
household iron, 36, 37
knives with disposable blades,
27, 28
linoleum knives, 28
paper cutters, 32
power tools, 33
punches, 33, 34, 35
rotary cutters, 31
scissors and snips, 32
scribing dividers, 39
straightedges, 25, 26, 27
toothed spreaders, 37, 38
veneer saws, 29, 30, 31
"Toothing" substrates, 72, 232, 233
Topcoats, 126
Trammel points, laying out with,
65, 66
Turnings, veneering, 117, 118
Urea-formaldehyde glue
characteristics of, 80, 81
cleaning up, 82
and initial adhesion, 75
laminating a press tabletop with,
106
mixing technique, 82, 163
Vacuum press, bonding with a, 99,
100–101, 102
Varnish, as topcoat, 126
Veneer
bonding to the substrate, 73–103

care after slicing, 17
cross-banded, 17
cutting, 53, 54
dyeing, 52
how it is cut, 14, 15, 16
how it is supplied, 17
paper-backed, 17
patching, 34, 35, 36
pieces, taping, 55, 56–57, 58
preforming, 52, 53
preparing, 43, 44–48, 49
presentations, 18, 19, 30
reason for using, 13, 14
repairing damages to, 43
shooting, 54, 55
"sizing," 51
species, characteristics of, 20,
21–24
strengthening, 50, 51, 52
taping, 55, 56–58
"Veneer-core" plywood, 63
Veneering
definition of, 12
history of, 12, 13
with a press, 96, 97, 98

Veneer saws
how to use, 29
modifying, 29, 30
shop-made, 30, 31
use in veneering, 28
Waffle board, 61
Walnut, and sun fade, 22
Water-based topcoats, 126
White glue
characteristics of, 80, 81
hardness of, 74
penetration characteristics of, 74
Window-cutting (marquetry), 131
Woodcarving tools, cutting veneer
with, 130, 232, 233
Wrinkles in veneer, 23
Yellow glue
characteristics of, 81
hardness of, 74
and initial tack, 75
penetration characteristics of, 74
Zebrawood
use as veneer, 14
using on desk, 174, 190, 191
using on dining table, 200, 210

METRIC CONVERSION CHART

MM=Millemeters CM=Centimeters

Inches	MM	CM	Inches	CM
⅛	3	0.3	4	10.2
¼	6	0.6	4½	11.4
⅜	10	1.0	5	12.7
½	13	1.3	6	15.2
⅝	16	1.6	7	17.8
¾	19	1.9	8	20.3
⅞	22	2.2	9	22.9
1	25	2.5	10	25.4
1¼	32	3.2	11	27.9
1½	38	3.8	12	30.5
1¾	44	4.4	13	33.0
2	51	5.1	14	35.6
2½	64	6.4	15	38.1
3	76	7.6	16	40.6
3½	89	8.9		